STEEPLE MESA TRAIL #73

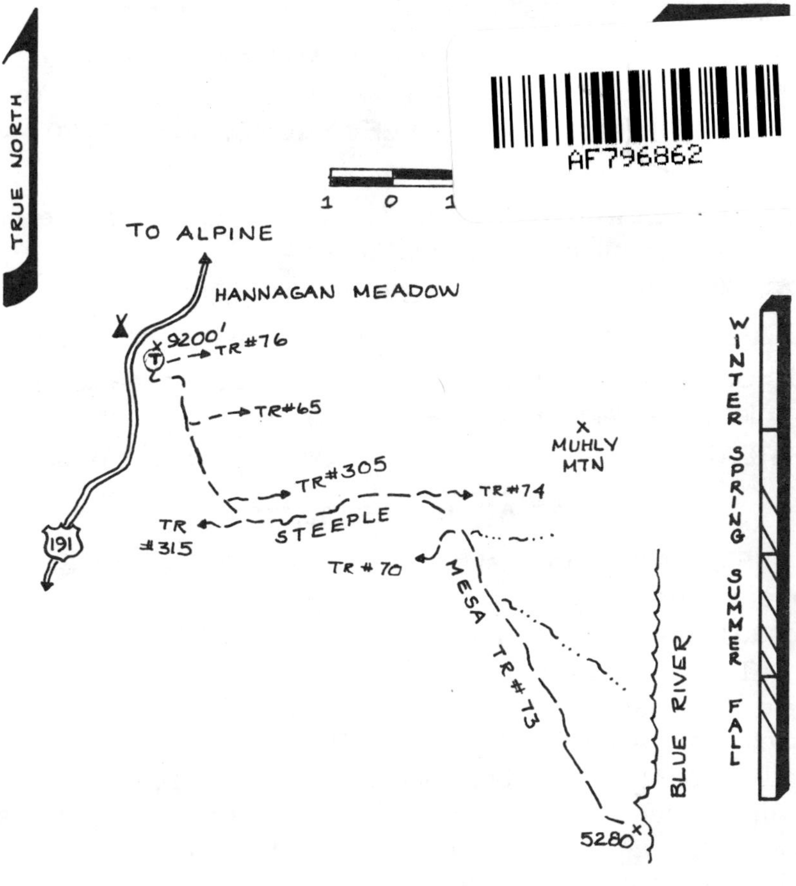

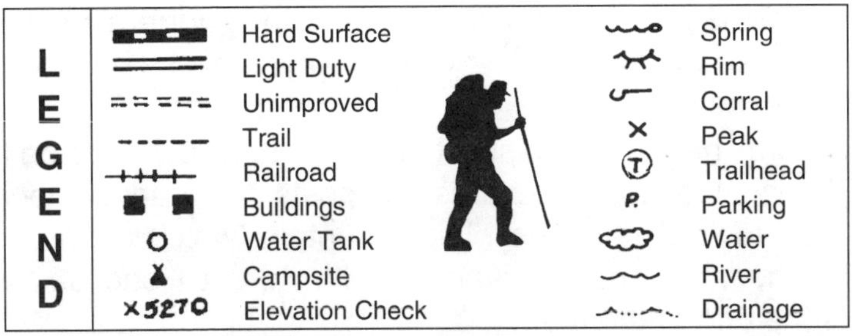

APACHE MAID TRAIL #15

ATTRACTION: Views down the canyon of Wet Beaver Creek, the Verde Valley and the Red Rock country of Sedona; solitude.

REQUIREMENTS: Lots of water and food, sturdy boots, proper maps; car okay to trailhead; 4.5 hours hiking time one way.

LOCATION: Beaver Creek Ranger Dist. - Wet Beaver Wilderness; 2 mi. sw of Sedona interchange off I-17 at F.R. 618A.

DIFFICULTY: Moderate **ELEVATIONS:** 4040' - 6420'

LENGTH: 9.5 miles one way.

MAPS REQUIRED: U.S.G.S. 7.5 min. topographic for Apache Maid Mountain and Casner Butte.

PERMIT: No **BIKES:** No, wilderness area.

EQUESTRIAN: Yes **WATER:** Best to bring your own.

INFORMATION: Trail is steep from the start but gets easier as you leave the wilderness area.

FIREARMS: Yes **PETS ON LEASH:** Preferred

TRAIL INFORMATION

From I-17, turn east on Forest Road 618 at the Sedona interchange. Drive approximately 2 miles and turn left onto Forest Road 618A. Continue 1/4 mile to trailhead at the end of road.

This trail leaves the Bell Trail #13 two miles east of parking lot and switchbacks its way to the top of the Mogollon Rim. This section of the trail is within the Wet Beaver wilderness. Once on top of the Rim the trail becomes more level and offers fine views of the surrounding country. Wet Beaver Creek with its lush riparian vegetation can be seen as it winds towards the Verde River. The Black Hills form a background for the Verde Valley to the southwest. The Red Rock country of Sedona is visible to the west and the majestic San Francisco Peaks rise on the northern horizon. To the south lies the Wet Beaver Creek canyon over 1200 feet deep and a mile across.

The trail becomes indistinct and hard to follow once on top of the Rim, but look for rock cairns and posts that mark the location. Continue towards Apache Maid Mountain, which looms on the eastern horizon, and the junction with Forest Road 620 which marks the end of the trail.

APACHE MAID TRAIL #15

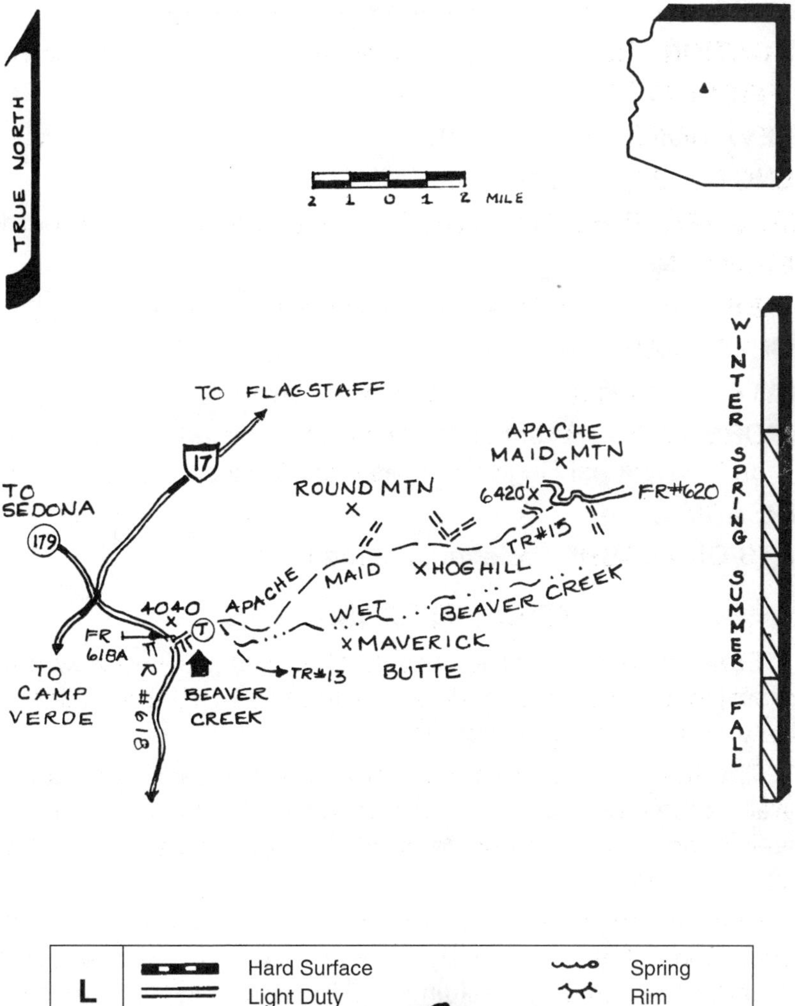

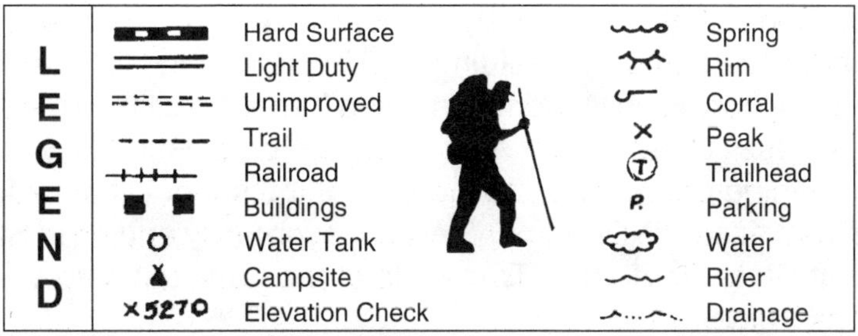

FLUME ROAD TRAIL #154

ATTRACTION: Nice Rim country views; nice family hike.

REQUIREMENTS: Water, lunch, sturdy boots, proper maps; car okay to trailhead; 1.5 hours hiking time one way.

LOCATION: Beaver Creek Ranger District west of Strawberry

DIFFICULTY: Easy

ELEVATIONS: 3800' - 4240'

LENGTH: 3.5 miles one way.

MAPS REQUIRED: U.S.G.S. 7.5 min. topographic for Strawberry.

PERMIT: No

BIKES: Yes, but not past dam into wilderness area.

EQUESTRIAN: Yes

WATER: Yes - but bring some of your own.

INFORMATION: Be sure not to walk on, or disturb, the flume; it's on the National Register of Historic Places.

FIREARMS: Yes

PETS ON LEASH: Preferred, not required

TRAIL INFORMATION

From Arizona State Highway 87 at Strawberry, turn west onto Forest Road 708 and continue approximately 14 miles to trailhead, located east of Irving power plant.

The trail starts across the creek from the parking area and parallels the creek for a short distance before climbing out of the creek bottom and passing through a gate. Please be sure to reclose the gate.

The trail begins its ascent of the hillside and junctions with Flume Road after approximately 1/4 mile, then heads east, passing under the flume several times. The Mogollon Rim forms the cliffs to the north and Deadman's Mesa forms the cliffs to the south across Fossil Creek. After about 1 mile, Forest Road 708 can be seen clinging precariously to the side of the sheer cliff face to the south as it ascends Deadman's Mesa, eventually ending in Strawberry at State Route 87. Trail ends at the dam just below Fossil Springs Wilderness.

FLUME ROAD TRAIL #154

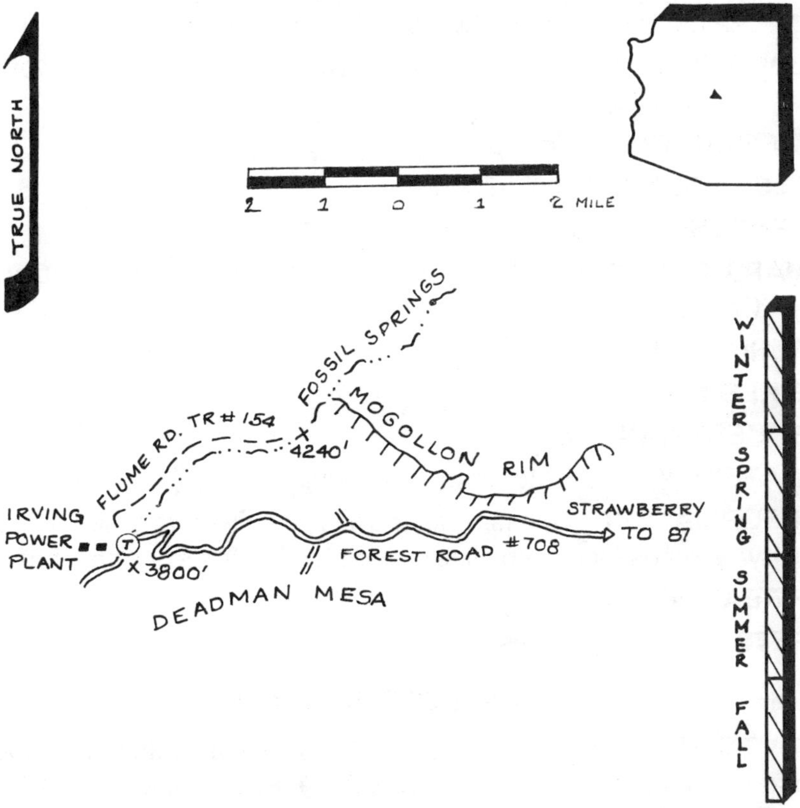

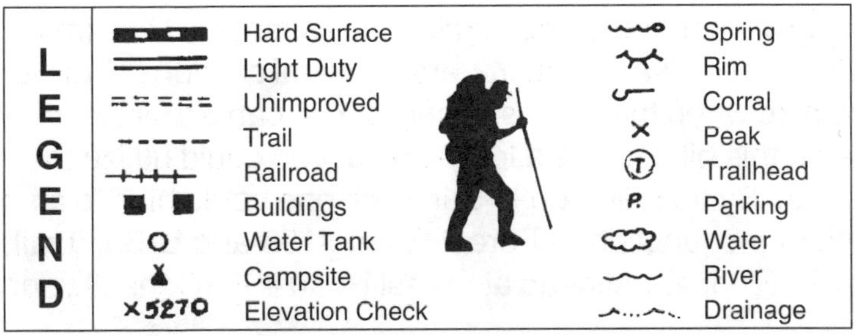

BARBERSHOP TRAIL #91

ATTRACTION: Many species of plants, lots of wildlife including bear and other large game.

REQUIREMENTS: Food, water, sturdy boots, proper maps; car okay to trailhead; 2.5 hours hiking time one way.

LOCATION: Blue Ridge Ranger District - Coconino National Forest.

DIFFICULTY: Moderate

ELEVATIONS: 7600' - 7250'

LENGTH: 4.5 miles one way.

MAPS REQUIRED: U.S.G.S. 7.5 min. topographic for Dane Canyon.

PERMIT: No

BIKES: No

EQUESTRIAN: Yes

WATER: Yes - best to bring your own.

INFORMATION: This is a good trail from which to build. Study your maps for possibilities including other trails or a car shuttle.

FIREARMS: Yes

PETS ON LEASH: Yes

TRAIL INFORMATION

Take Forest Highway #3 (Lake Mary Road) south of Flagstaff about 55 miles to the junction of AZ 87. Travel northeast on AZ 87 to Forest Road #95 (about 9 miles), just past the Blue Ridge Campground turnoff. Turn right (south) and continue to the junction of Forest Road #139 (about 8 miles). Take Forest Road #139 south. Watch for the trailhead on your left (6.5 to 7 miles).

You will not find steep climbs or descents on this trail. It is a pleasant open hike as you traverse several canyons. This is really a nice hike when the leaves change. You can either return as you came on this hike or, for a longer hike, you could utilize the U-Bar Trail #28. By traveling on U-Bar Trail, one could hike to a second car left at the junction of Forest Road #139 and U-Bar Trail, or at U-Bar Trail upper trailhead at Forest Road #95. Consult your map.

BARBERSHOP TRAIL #91

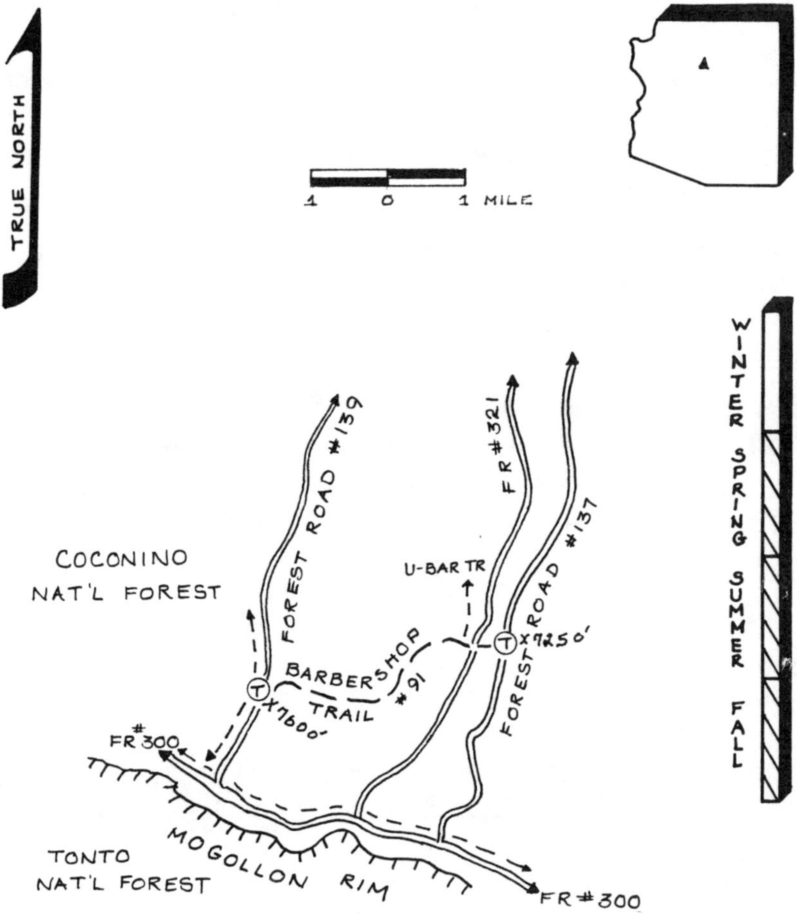

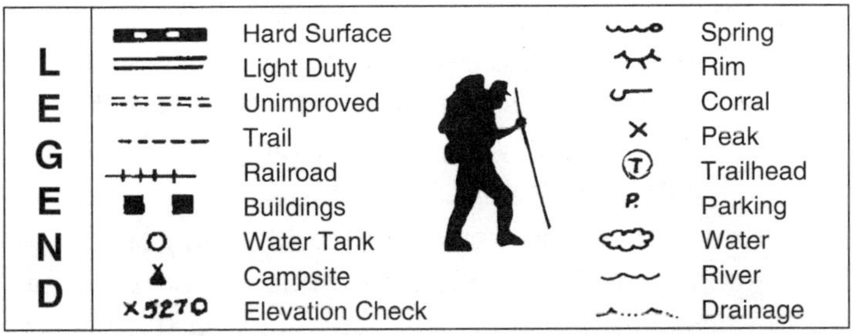

U-BAR TRAIL #28

ATTRACTION: Nice forest areas as well as canyons and grasslands, many species of plants, lots of wildlife.

REQUIREMENTS: Food, water, sturdy boots, proper maps; car okay to trailhead; 4.5 hours hiking time one way.

LOCATION: Blue Ridge Ranger District - Coconino National Forest.

DIFFICULTY: Moderate to Difficult

ELEVATIONS: 7750' - 7250'

LENGTH: 6.5 miles one way.

MAPS REQUIRED: U.S.G.S. 7.5 min. topographic for Dane Canyon.

PERMIT: No

BIKES: No

WATER: No - bring your own.

EQUESTRIAN: Yes

INFORMATION: Some portions are difficult as you must follow blazes on trees as no trail is evident; not for a novice.

FIREARMS: Yes

PETS ON LEASH: Yes

TRAIL INFORMATION

Take Forest Highway #3 (Lake Mary Rd.) south of Flagstaff about 55 miles to the junction of AZ Rt. 87 at Clint's Well. Take AZ 87 north about 9 miles to Forest Road #95, turn right (south) and follow 11-12 miles to the junction of Fred Haugt Trail #22, Houston Brothers Trail #18 and the upper trailhead of U-Bar Trail #28. It's on the left side of Forest Road #95 just before it hairpins and heads south.

Trail heads southeast from the start. Be prepared to take your time and get used to following cairns and tree blazes as, in some areas, you will be depending on them to find your way. At about the 2-mile mark, you will cross Forest Road #139. Prepare for rock cliffs above as well as rich grassy areas. At the 4-mile mark a few switchbacks will begin, then you will travel due south to the end of the trail at the junction of Barbershop Trail #91.

Either return the same way or turn right (west) on Barbershop Trail to a second car at its western trailhead at Forest Road #139. These two trails work well together. Consult your map.

U-BAR TRAIL #28

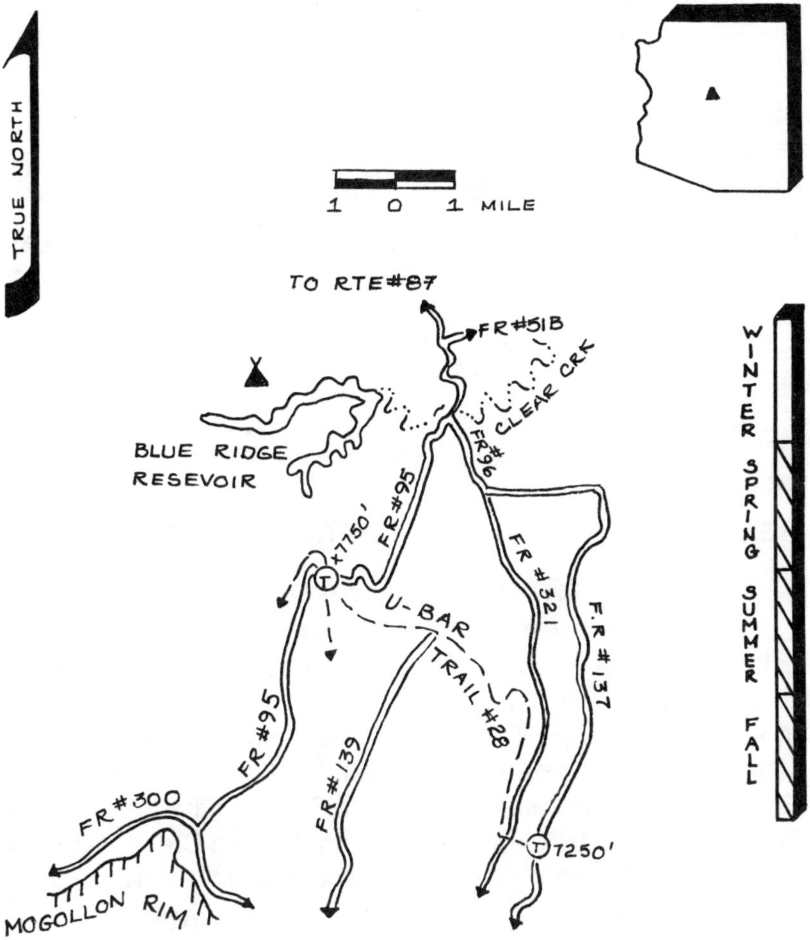

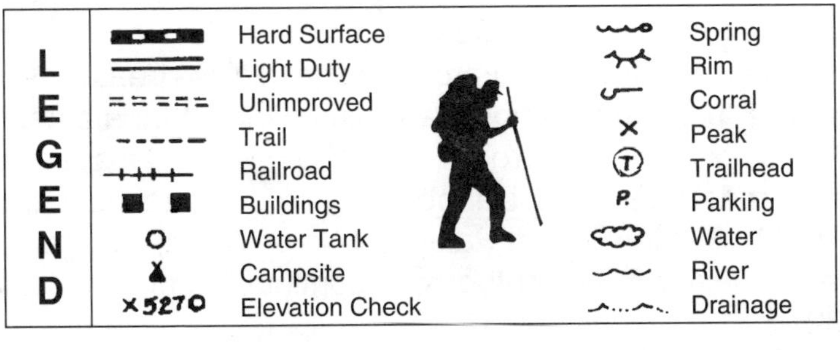

E CROSS L TRAIL #281

ATTRACTION: From Ash Creek Ridge are views to the south of Crook's Canyon and Mt. Union.

REQUIREMENTS: Lots of water, food, sturdy boots, rain gear, maps; high clearance vehicle to trailhead; 5 hours hiking time round trip.

LOCATION: Bradshaw Ranger District, 13 miles south of Prescott.

DIFFICULTY: Moderate

ELEVATIONS: 6900' - 5800' **LENGTH:** 4.8 miles one way.

MAPS REQUIRED: Prescott National Forest map, west half; U.S.G.S. topographic 7.5' quads for Battleship Butte and Groom Creek.

PERMIT: No **BIKES:** Yes **EQUESTRIAN:** Yes

WATER: Not dependable - bring your own.

INFORMATION: Occasional pools of water for horses. Palace Station served as a stage stop until 1910. It's now a Forest Service Administrative Site.

FIREARMS: Yes **PETS ON LEASH:** Yes

TRAIL INFORMATION

The northern access is preferred, particularly by hikers, since it is the highest elevation. To reach trailhead, take the Senator Highway (F.R. 52) south from Prescott for about 11 miles to the turnoff to Mt. Union (F.R. 261). Continue south on F.R. 52 for .3 mile to F.R. 52B. Take this road west for .3 mile to junction with F.R. 81. Follow this south for another .3 mile to the junction with F.R. 70. Take F.R. 70 southeast along the Ash Creek Ridge for about .4 mile to trailhead on the right. Trailhead may not be signed.

From Ash Creek Ridge, the trail drops south into the Ash Creek drainage and follows the creek for 2.3 miles. You will pass two potential sources of water: Quail Spring and E Cross L Spring. Water cannot be depended on. Do not drink unless treated. At mile 2.3, the trail turns sharply northeast climbing another drainage for 1.2 miles back to the Ash Creek Ridge and F.R. 70. This part of the trail is the most difficult. It is another 1 mile to where the trail ends on F.R. 52, .2 mile north of Palace Station. Where the trail turns northeast in Ash Creek, another spur continues south for .4 mile to F.R. 82.

E CROSS L TRAIL #281

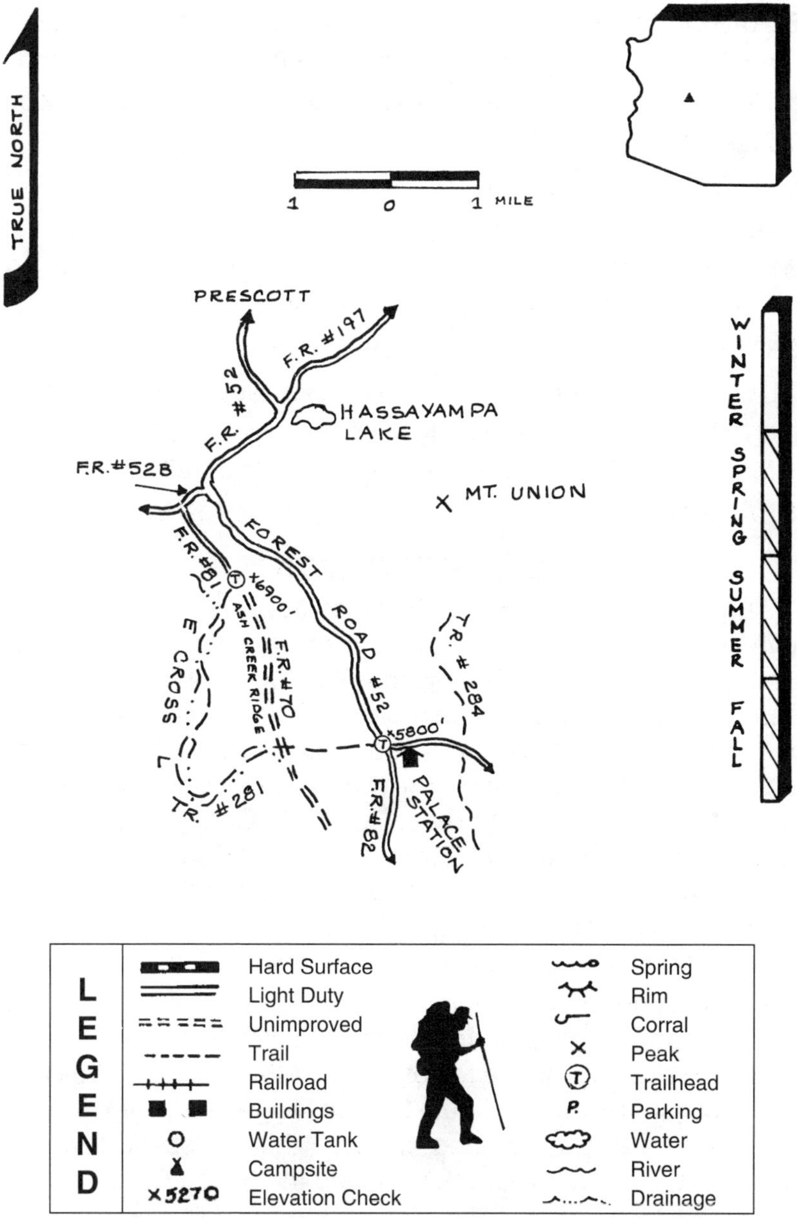

GROOM CREEK LOOP TRAIL #307

ATTRACTION: Ponderosa pine areas with views of the Crown King area, Prescott area, Mingus Mountain, and on a clear day, the San Francisco Peaks.

REQUIREMENTS: Lots of water, food, sturdy boots, rain gear, maps; car okay to trailheads; 6 hours hiking time round trip.

LOCATION: Bradshaw Ranger District, 6.5 miles south of Prescott.

DIFFICULTY: Difficult

ELEVATIONS: 6400' - 7700'

LENGTH: 8.7 miles round trip.

MAPS REQUIRED: Prescott National Forest, west half; U.S.G.S. topographic 7.5' quads for Groom Creek.

PERMIT: No

BIKES: Yes

EQUESTRIAN: Yes

WATER: No - bring your own.

INFORMATION: Hikers mostly start from picnic area on Spruce Mountain. No motorized equipment on this trail.

FIREARMS: Yes

PETS ON LEASH: Yes

TRAIL INFORMATION

The Groom Creek Horse Camp is approximately 6.5 miles south of Prescott on the Senator Highway (Forest Road 52). Hikers may also access the trail from the top of Spruce Mountain where there is a maintained picnic area. To access the trail at this point, from Prescott turn south onto Mount Vernon Avenue. This road becomes the Senator Highway and, once within the Prescott National Forest, becomes Forest Road 52. Continue south from Prescott for approximately 4.5 miles to Forest Road 52A (on east side of main road). You will have just passed the entrance to Goldwater Lake before coming to Forest Road 52A. Turn left onto Forest Road 52A and travel for about 4 miles to the picnic area.

From the north loop at the Horse Camp, the trail stays almost entirely in timber, climbing for about 2.8 miles through the upper Wolf Creek drainage to the top of Spruce Mountain. The trail then turns southwest down the South Spruce Ridge for about 1.6 miles. It then begins a long, twisting, almost 4-mile descent down the mountain to the Groom Creek area and the Horse Camp.

GROOM CREEK LOOP
TRAIL #307

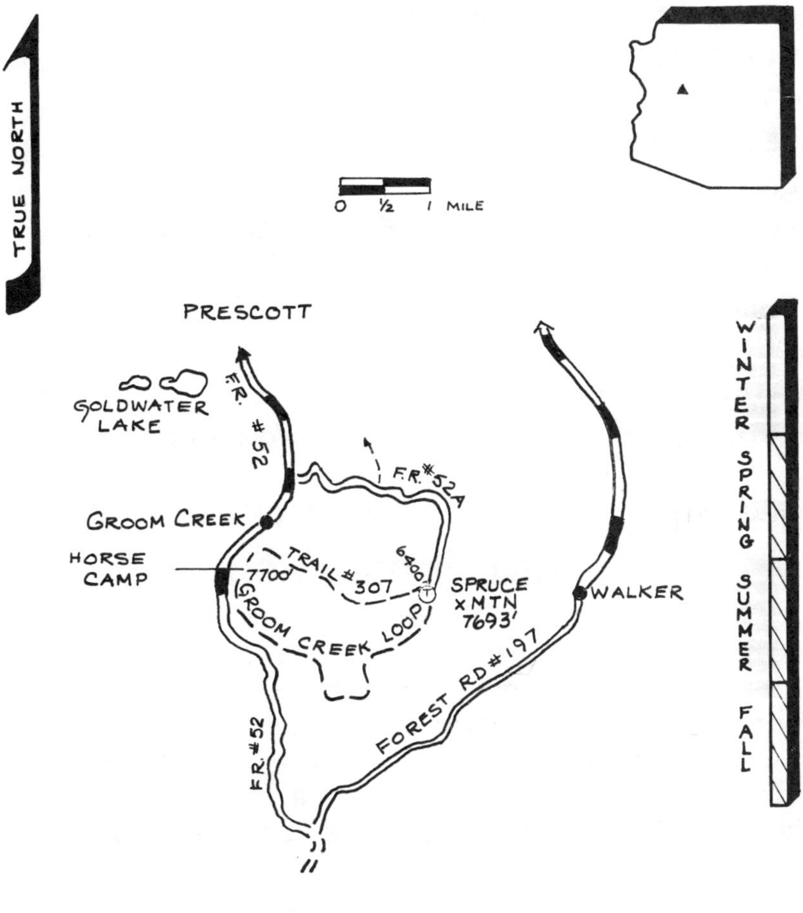

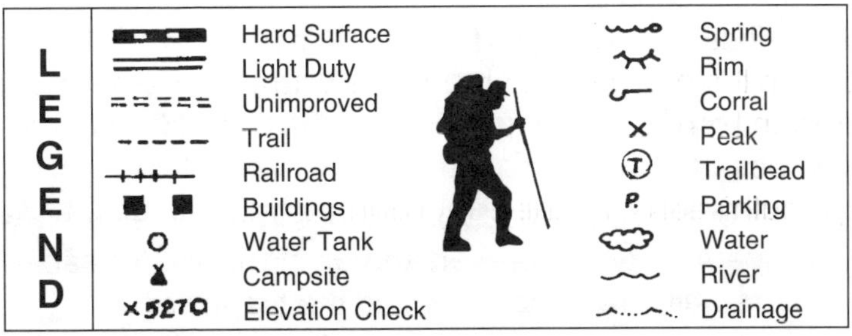

KENDRICK MOUNTAIN TRAIL #22

ATTRACTION: Views of Grand Canyon, Painted Desert, Snow Bowl, Sunset Crater.

REQUIREMENTS: Food, water, sturdy boots, proper maps; car okay to trailhead; 2.5 to 3 hours hiking time one way.

LOCATION: Chalender Ranger District, 16 miles west of Flagstaff.

DIFFICULTY: Moderate

ELEVATIONS: 7980' - 10,418'

LENGTH: 3.5 miles one way.

MAPS REQUIRED: U.S.G.S. 7.5 min. topographic for Kendrick Peak.

PERMIT: No

BIKES: No

EQUESTRIAN: Yes

WATER: No - bring your own.

INFORMATION: Severe storms develop quickly at this altitude. Note: Peak is at 10,418 feet. Pace yourself!

FIREARMS: Yes

PETS ON LEASH: Yes

TRAIL INFORMATION

From Flagstaff, take I-40 west to the Parks exit (16 miles) and turn right to a "T" intersection. Turn left and travel .4 mile to Spring Valley Road and turn right at the Union 76 station. Take Spring Valley Road 8 miles and turn onto Forest Road #194 (well marked). Take #194 about 4 miles to Forest Road #171 and turn right. Go 3 miles to Forest Road #171A, turn left and drive one mile to trailhead. After crossing through a small gate, the first mile of this trail follows an old road, with wide access and gentle switchbacks which, in just over a mile, turns into a spacious trail.

The trail is constantly uphill, clear to the top, through thinned-out ponderosa pine, Douglas fir, white fir, southwest white pine and corkbark fir. Stop and look around, there are more volcanic cinder cones than you can count and views of the Grand Canyon and the Painted Desert.

At the 10,000-foot level, you will reach a grassy area with a view that seems to go on forever, and an old fire-watch cabin. You are a quarter mile from the peak and the fire tower.

KENDRICK MOUNTAIN
TRAIL #22

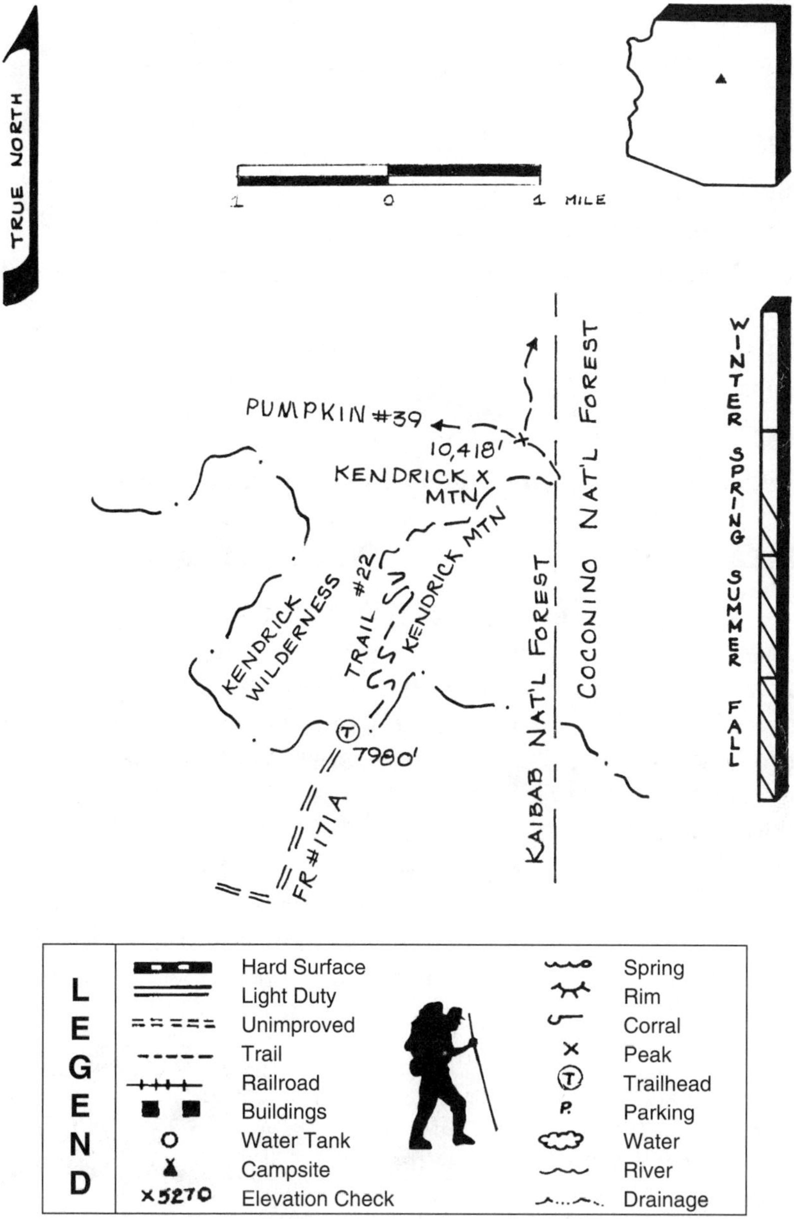

PUMPKIN TRAIL #39

ATTRACTION: Offers ridge hiking through woods and open meadows, fantastic views from the top.

REQUIREMENTS: Food, water, sturdy boots, proper maps; car okay to trailhead; 3 hours hiking time one way.

LOCATION: Chalender Ranger District - Kendrick Mountain, east of Williams.

DIFFICULTY: Moderate

ELEVATIONS: 7260' - 10,418'

LENGTH: 5.5 miles one way.

MAPS REQUIRED: U.S.G.S. 7.5 min. topographic for Moritz Ridge/Kendrick.

PERMIT: No **BIKES:** No

EQUESTRIAN: Yes

WATER: No - bring your own.

INFORMATION: Study your maps for alternate trails back down with possible car shuttle.

FIREARMS: Yes **PETS ON LEASH:** Yes

TRAIL INFORMATION

From Williams, take I-40 east to the Parks exit. Turn left across the overpass and continue north on Forest Road #141 for about 8 miles. Turn left onto Forest Road #144 and go about 4.5 miles to Forest Road #171. Turn right on Forest Road #171 and go 2.75 miles to the right angle curve in the road. Turn onto the dirt road (at the curve) and park at the trailhead.

The trail follows an old logging road, then climbs along a steep canyon. You will pass through a pole gate, ascend a ridge and begin heading southeast to an old helispot. The trail continues to follow this ridge through woods and open meadows to the top of Kendrick Mountain.

There are several alternate trails to use on the way back down. The remains of a herder's cabin are along the trail about 1/4 mile below the fire tower.

PUMPKIN TRAIL #39

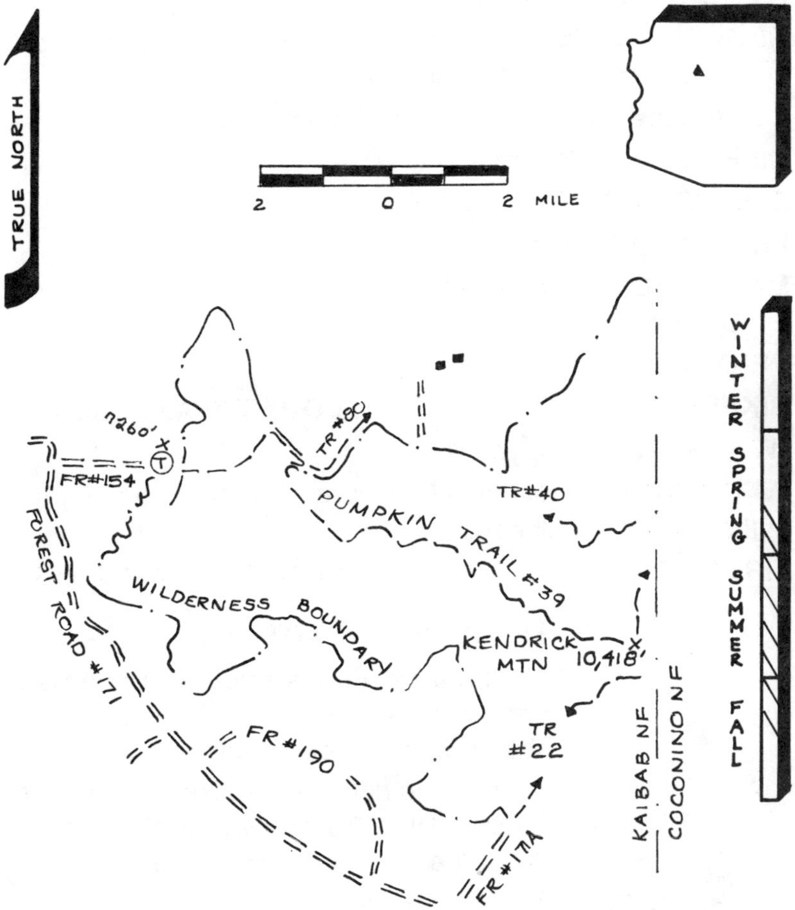

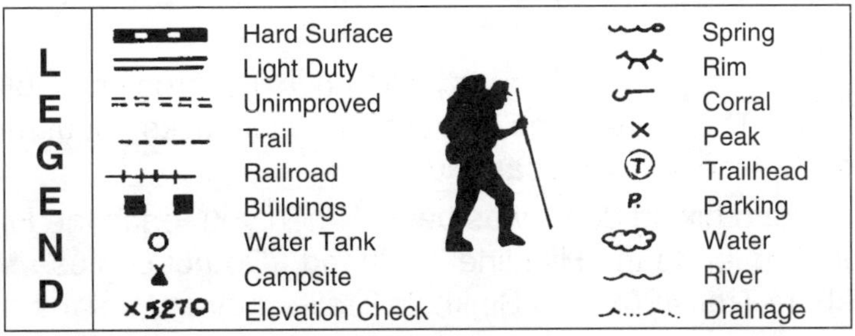

MILITARY SINKHOLE TRAIL #966

ATTRACTION: Nice views, cool.

REQUIREMENTS: Food, water, sturdy boots, proper maps; car okay to trailhead; 1 hour hiking time one way.

LOCATION: Chevelon Ranger District - Mogollon Rim.

DIFFICULTY: Moderate

ELEVATIONS: 7600' - 6750'

LENGTH: 1.5 miles one way.

MAPS REQUIRED: U.S.G.S. 7.5 min. topographic for Woods Canyon.

PERMIT: No

BIKES: No **EQUESTRIAN:** Yes

WATER: No - bring your own.

INFORMATION: Nice trail for horses. Plenty of room for trailers at the S.R. 260 trailhead.

FIREARMS: Yes **PETS ON LEASH:** Yes

TRAIL INFORMATION

If you hike up this trail, the trailhead is at the Highline trailhead on State Rt. 260, 1 1/4 miles above Colcord Road, north of Payson.

If hiking down, the trailhead can be found via State Rt. 260 out of Payson all the way to the top of the Rim. Turn left on Rim Road (#300) and travel about 1 mile to a paved parking area on your left. The trailhead is at the west end of this lot.

You should have no problems following this trail. There are some interesting switchbacks about midway. This is a nice trail for a car shuttle.

I found hiking down was best. When you reach the Highline Trail, turn left to the Highline Trailhead. Do not confuse Military Sinkhole Trail #966 with Sinkhole Trail—they are not the same!

MILITARY SINKHOLE TRAIL #966

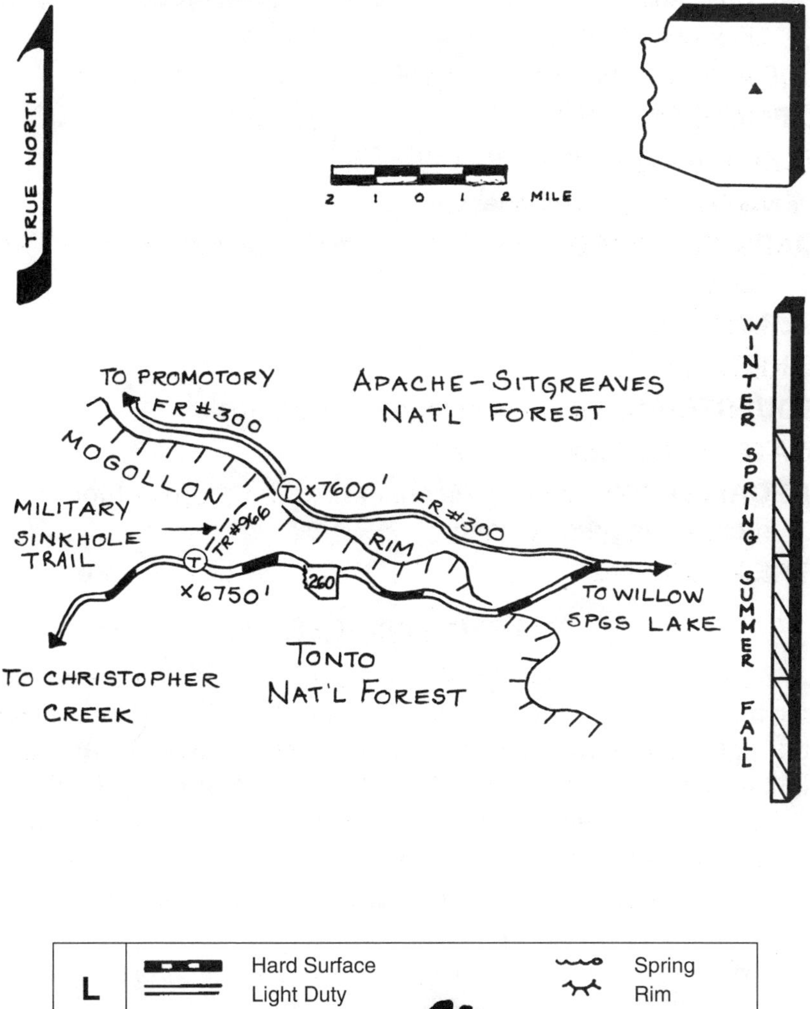

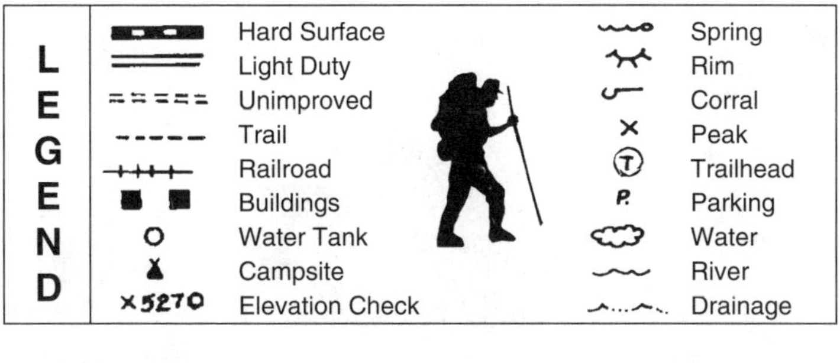

TELEPHONE RIDGE TRAIL #103

ATTRACTION: Nice views, unusual scenery and plantlife, solitude.

REQUIREMENTS: Food, water, sturdy boots, proper maps; car okay to trailhead; 1.5 hours hiking time one way.

LOCATION: Chevelon Ranger District - Chevelon Canyon.

DIFFICULTY: Difficult

ELEVATIONS: 7200' - 6500'

LENGTH: 1.25 miles one way.

MAPS REQUIRED: U.S.G.S. 7.5 min. topographic for Woods Canyon.

PERMIT: No

BIKES: No

EQUESTRIAN: Not recommended - loose rock.

WATER: No - bring your own.

INFORMATION: Very challenging hike; be prepared for loose rock, some brush cutting.

FIREARMS: Yes **PETS ON LEASH:** Yes

TRAIL INFORMATION

Take State Rt. 260 out of Payson to the top of the Mogollon Rim and turn left on Rim Road (#300). Take #300 to Forest Road #169, turn right, take Forest Road #169 to Forest Road #119 and turn right again. The trailhead is at the end of Forest Road #119.

Just south of the lake, you start descending into Chevelon Canyon with fine views into the canyon. Be careful as you encounter loose rock and downed trees as you descend to the trail's end at Chevelon Creek.

This trail is a great test of your abilities. Return the same way.

TELEPHONE RIDGE TRAIL #103

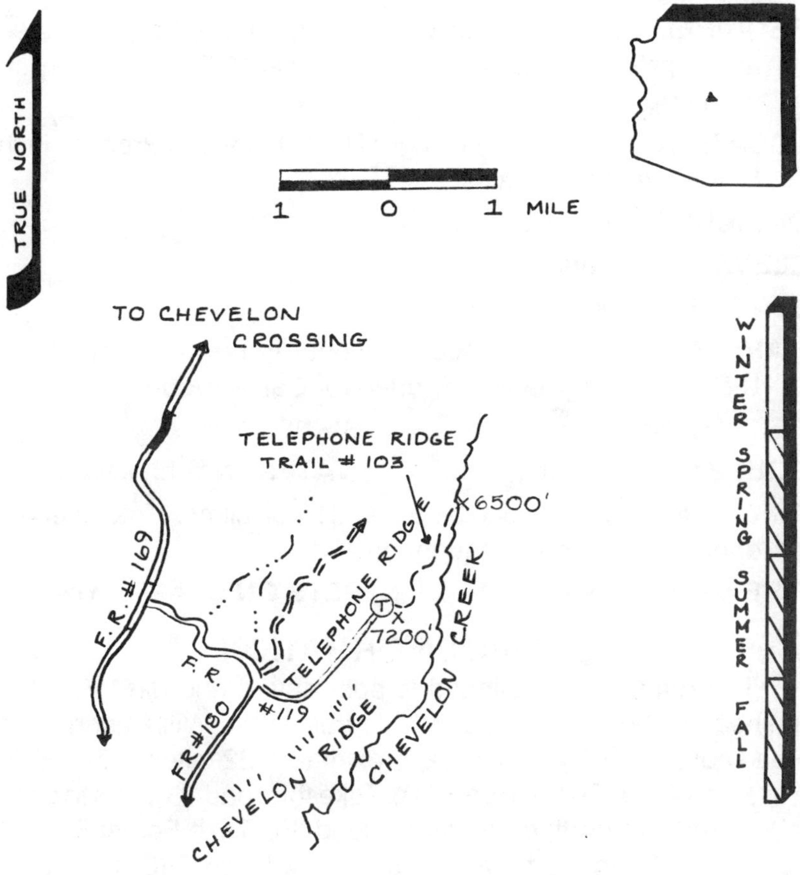

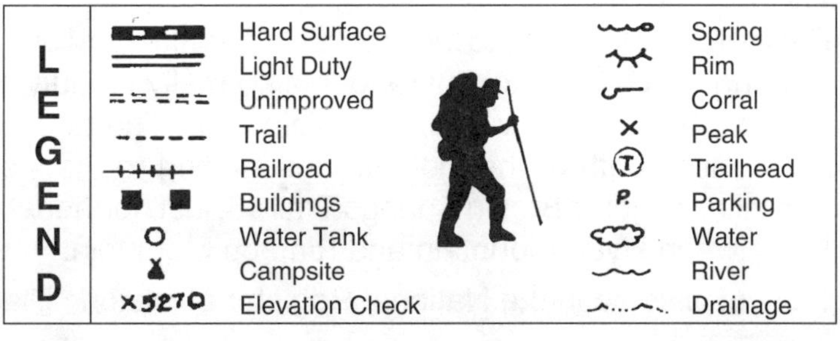

HYDE MOUNTAIN TRAIL #6

ATTRACTION: Trail is primarily a service road to Hyde Mountain Lookout. Lookout is highest point in Santa Maria Mountains and offers fine views.

REQUIREMENTS: Lots of water, food, sturdy boots for steep areas, proper maps; car okay to trailhead; 2.5 hours hiking time round trip.

LOCATION: Chino Valley Ranger District, north of Prescott in the Santa Maria Mountains.

DIFFICULTY: Difficult

ELEVATIONS: 5880' - 7272'

LENGTH: 2 miles one way.

MAPS REQUIRED: Prescott National Forest map, west half; U.S.G.S. topographic 7.5' quad for Camp Wood.

PERMIT: No

BIKES: Yes

EQUESTRIAN: Yes

WATER: No - bring your own.

INFORMATION: This can be a hot, difficult climb. Take plenty of drinking water and frequent breaks.

FIREARMS: Yes

PETS ON LEASH: Yes

TRAIL INFORMATION

The road to the trailhead is both paved and dirt. The east trailhead is the main access to this trail. Take Williamson Valley Road north from Prescott for approximately 22 miles to the turnoff to Camp Wood (Forest Road 21). Take this road 16 miles to Camp Wood and turn north onto Forest Road 95. Take Forest Road 95 about .3 mile and turn west onto Forest Road 95C, then travel approximately 1.75 miles to the trailhead near the end of this road. Parking is limited as is turn-around space.

The trail climbs directly to the lookout. The latter third of the trail is steep and difficult. A lookout ranger is normally on duty during May, June and July and visitors are welcome. The trail divides about 1/4 mile south of the lookout, descending to the west for about .8 mile and joins Brown Springs Trail #5, just northeast of the saddle between Hyde Mountain and Pinetop Mountain.

The lookout is listed in the National Register of Historic Places.

HYDE MOUNTAIN TRAIL #6

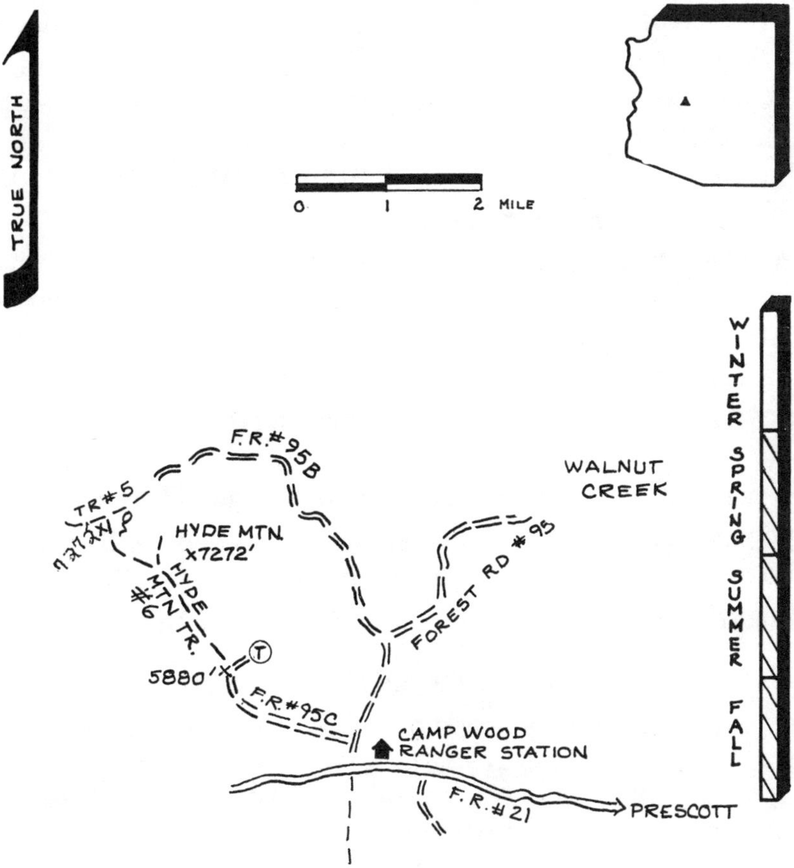

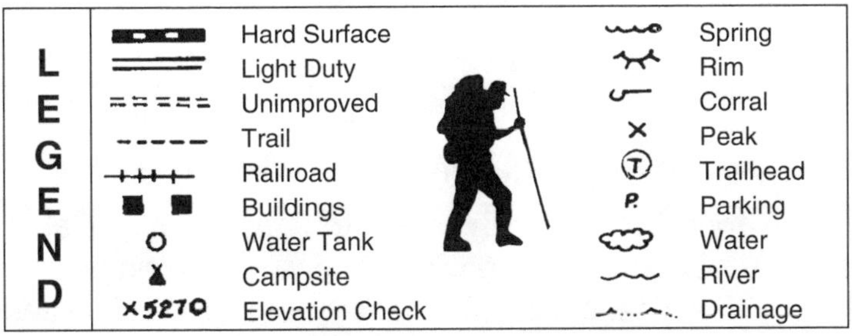

SYCAMORE TRAIL #63

ATTRACTION: Trail offers spectacular views of Sycamore Canyon and surrounding Red Rock Bluffs.

REQUIREMENTS: Lots of water, food, rain gear, sturdy boots, proper maps; high clearance vehicle to get to trailhead; 9 hours hiking time round trip.

LOCATION: Chino Valley Ranger District, northeast of Chino Valley in the Sycamore Canyon Wilderness.

DIFFICULTY: Moderate **ELEVATIONS:** 4700' - 4500'

LENGTH: 11.2 miles to Trail #70.

MAPS REQUIRED: Prescott (east half) and Coconino National Forest maps; U.S.G.S. topographic 7.5' quads for Sycamore Basin, Loy Butte, and Sycamore Point.

PERMIT: No - maximum group size of 25.

BIKES: No **EQUESTRIAN:** Yes

WATER: No dependable water on this trail during summer. Winter flows can be heavy. Not recommended for summer.

INFORMATION: Trail offers spectacular views of Sycamore Canyon and surrounding Red Rock Bluffs.

FIREARMS: Yes **PETS ON LEASH:** Yes

TRAIL INFORMATION

Hike starts at the junction of Trail #53 and the end of Forest Road 181. From Chino Valley, take the Perkinsville Road (Forest Road 354) approximately 23 miles to Forest Road 181; take this road east about 6 miles to Henderson Flat; continue southeast for another 5 miles to the Sycamore Canyon Wilderness boundary.

The lower section of the trail is relatively level through Sycamore Basin at an elevation of about 4500 ft. The trail approaches Sycamore Creek at about mile 5 and, from there, stays either in, or close to, the canyon bottom until about mile 11.2. Here the trail becomes Coconino National Forest Trail #70 and leaves the wilderness, climbing over 2000 ft. to Winter Cabin.

As you approach it from the south trailhead, Taylor Cabin is at about mile 9. Once used as a winter line camp, it is now listed on the National Register of Historic Places, but is open to visitor use.

SYCAMORE TRAIL #63

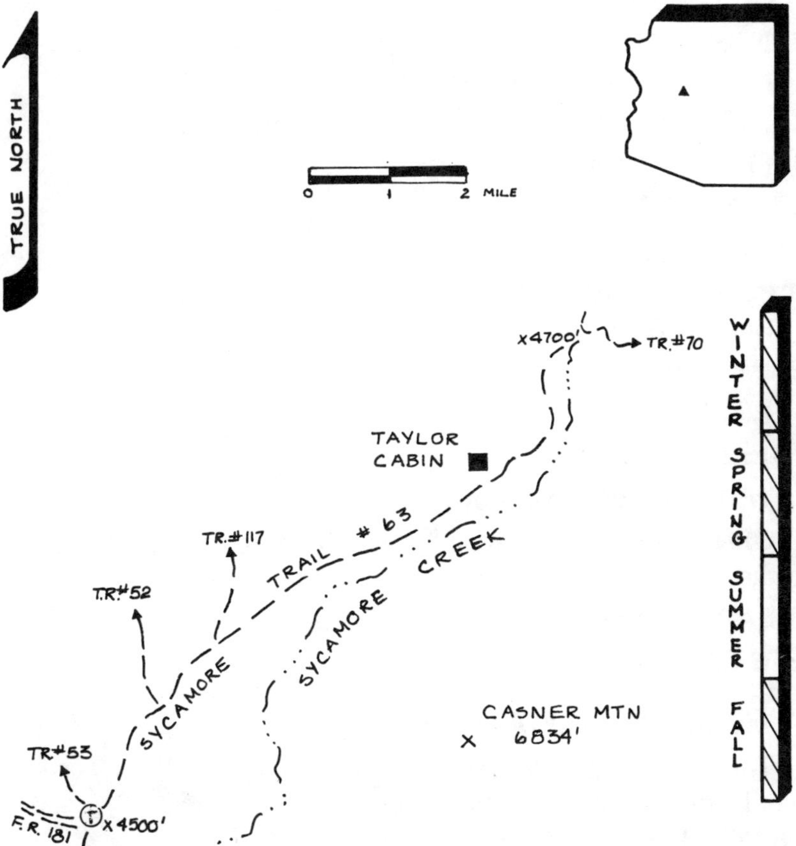

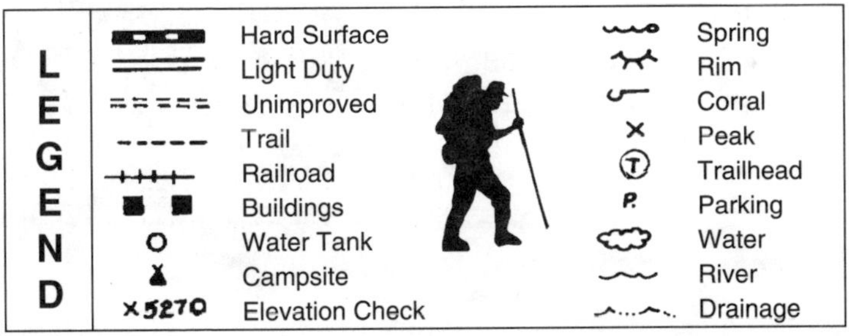

RIM LAKES VISTA TRAIL #622

ATTRACTION: Easy hiking, unmatched views.

REQUIREMENTS: Food, water, sturdy boots, proper maps; car okay to trailhead; 3 hours hiking time round trip.

LOCATION: Heber Ranger District - Mogollon Rim.

DIFFICULTY: Easy

ELEVATIONS: 7600'

LENGTH: 3.5 miles one way.

MAPS REQUIRED: U.S.G.S. 7.5 min. topographic for Woods Canyon SW.

PERMIT: No

BIKES: Yes

EQUESTRIAN: Yes

WATER: No - bring your own.

INFORMATION: Take care if the weather threatens as the Rim is the second most lightning-struck area on earth.

FIREARMS: Yes

PETS ON LEASH: Yes

TRAIL INFORMATION

Take State Rt. 260 southwest from Heber 26 miles to the Rim Road #300 and head west on Rim Road approximately 3/4 mile to the Mogollon Campground where you will find the trailhead.

The trail basically heads west along the Rim. This trail speaks for itself—what scenery!

RIM LAKES VISTA
TRAIL #622

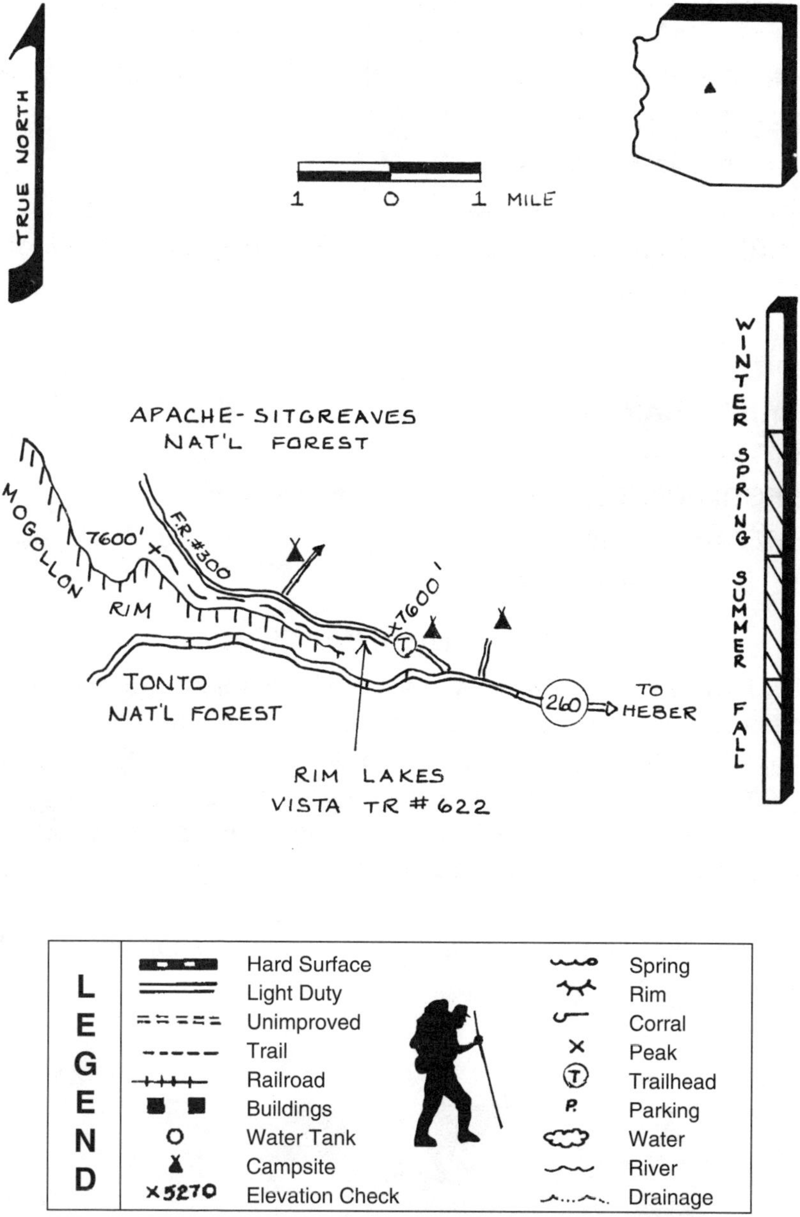

SINKHOLE TRAIL

ATTRACTION: A chance to relive some history and to experience the uniqueness of the sinkhole itself.

REQUIREMENTS: Food, water, sturdy boots, proper maps; car okay to trailhead; .5 hour hiking time each way.

LOCATION: Heber Ranger District - Canyon Point Campground.

DIFFICULTY: Easy

ELEVATIONS: 7600' - 7500'

LENGTH: .5 mile one way

MAPS REQUIRED: U.S.G.S. 7.5 min. topographic for Woods Canyon SE.

PERMIT: No

BIKES: No

EQUESTRIAN: Yes

WATER: No

INFORMATION: An easy trail for a family hike.

FIREARMS: Yes

PETS ON LEASH: Yes

TRAIL INFORMATION

Take State Rt. 260 southwest of Heber for approximately 17 miles and take the turnoff to Canyon Point Campground. The trailhead is at Loop B in the campground.

The trail follows an old road, and at about midway the trail heads west. Soon you will be at the edge of the sinkhole itself. It was drained by a fissure that appeared years ago. The trail ends at the sinkhole.

How many different plant forms and sounds can you identify while in the sinkhole?

SINKHOLE TRAIL

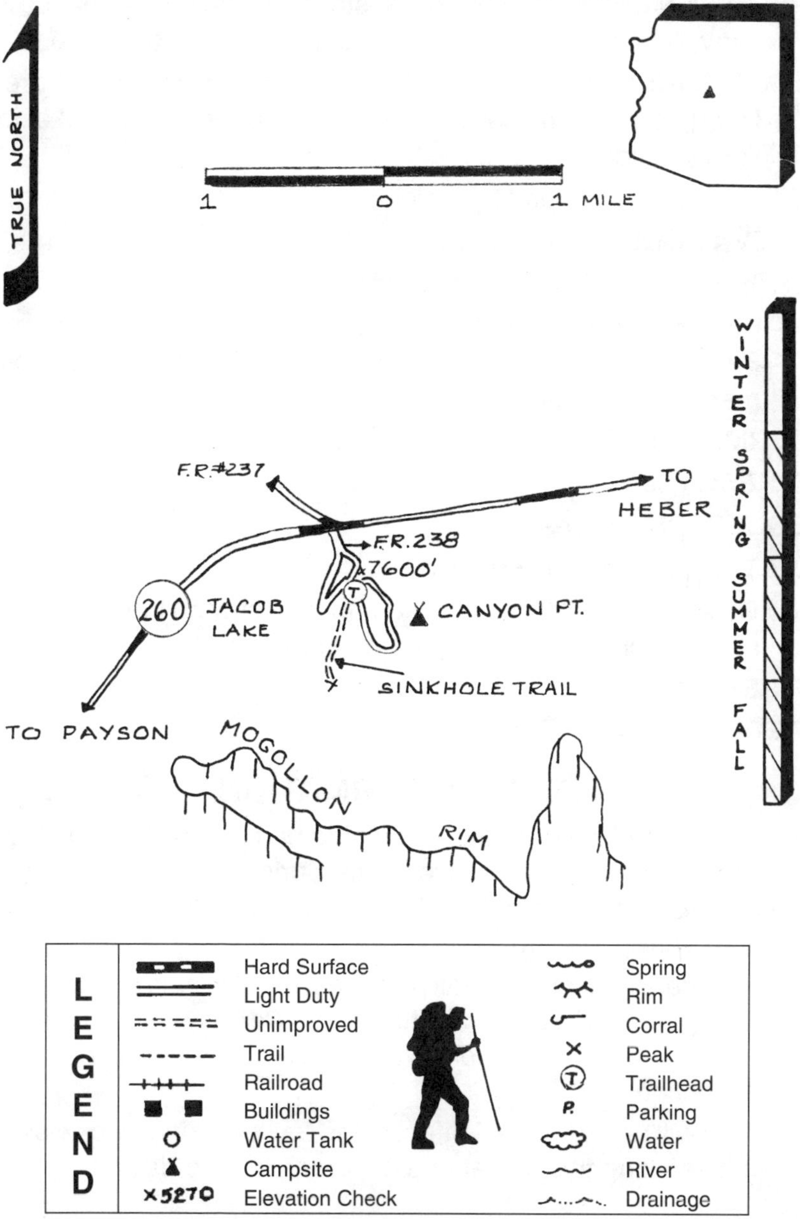

SPRINGS LOOP TRAIL #633

ATTRACTION: Follows Thompson Creek for a distance, then through meadows and pines.

REQUIREMENTS: Water, snack, sturdy boots, proper maps; car okay to trailhead; 1.75 hours total hiking time round trip.

LOCATION: Lakeside Ranger District trailhead located on Forest Road 182, 1.9 miles from Highway 260 south of Lakeside Ranger Station.

DIFFICULTY: Moderate - rocky terrain.

ELEVATIONS: 7000' - 7200'

LENGTH: 3.8 miles one way.

MAPS REQUIRED: District map available at District Office, Pinetop/Lakeside Parks & Recreation Dept.; Chamber of Commerce Forest map.

PERMIT: No

BIKES: Yes

EQUESTRIAN: Yes

WATER: No - bring your own.

INFORMATION: Difficult for bikes - please stay on the trail. Areas near the creek and springs are very fragile.

FIREARMS: Yes

PETS ON LEASH: Yes

TRAIL INFORMATION

Travel east from Pinetop-Lakeside on Highway 260 and turn left at Pinetop Lakes entrance (Buck Springs Road). Go .6 mile and turn left onto road to Sky Hi Retreat (Forest Road 182). Go 1.3 miles to entrance to trailhead on left.

The trail area contains tall pine, oak, creeks, springs, sensitive riparian areas, and varied wildlife. The trail is easy walking through new trail and old road sections with little gain in elevation, but some rocky sections.

You will enjoy the best effect of the trail by hiking clockwise. A quiet hike along this trail above the creek is pure delight. A nice family hike.

SPRINGS LOOP TRAIL #633

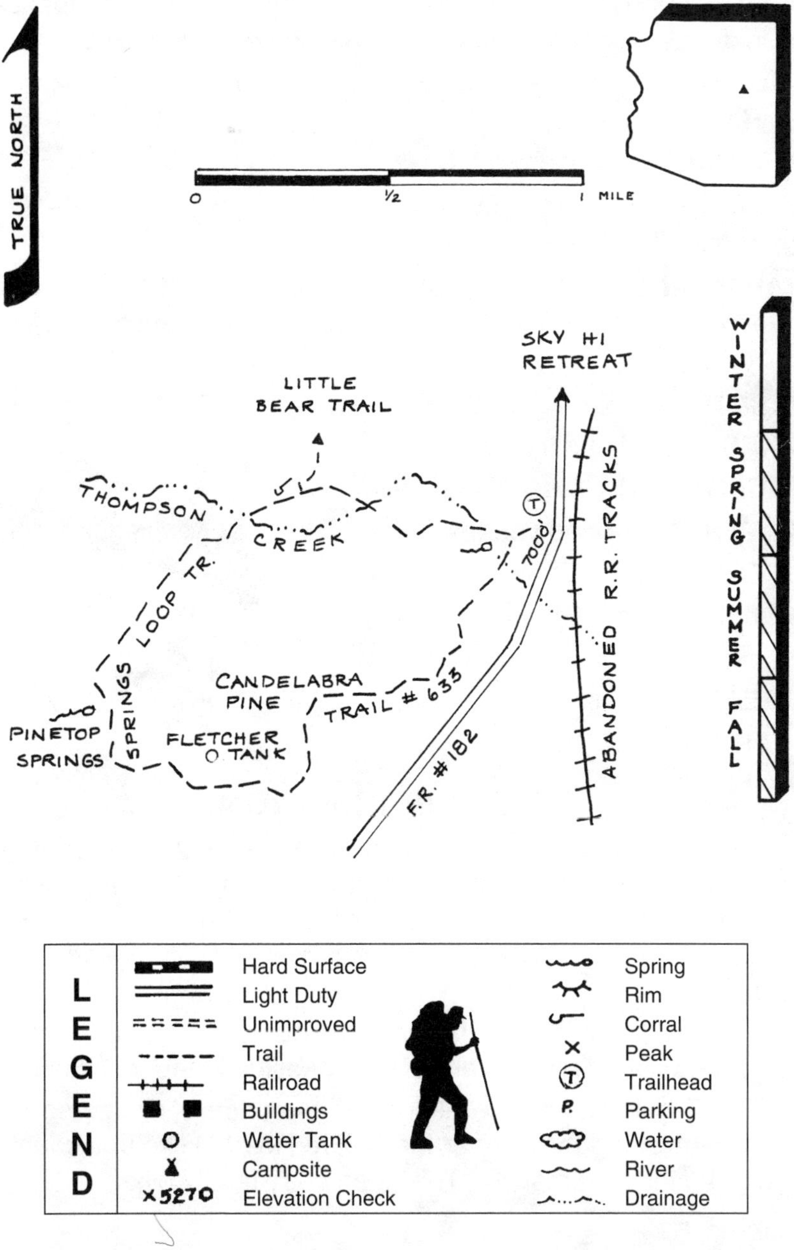

TIMBER MESA TRAIL #636

ATTRACTION: Views from trail of Jacques Marsh, Lakeside and distant mountains.

REQUIREMENTS: Water, food, sturdy boots, proper maps; car okay to trailhead; 3 hours total hiking time round trip.

LOCATION: Lakeside Ranger District; due east of Lakeside Ranger Station.

DIFFICULTY: Moderate

ELEVATIONS: 6600' - 6900'

LENGTH: 6 miles round trip.

MAPS REQUIRED: District map available at District Office, Pinetop/Lakeside Parks & Recreation Dept.; Chamber of Commerce Forest map.

PERMIT: No

BIKES: Yes, but difficult

EQUESTRIAN: Yes

WATER: No - bring your own.

INFORMATION: Trailhead can be muddy and also difficult for turning around horse trailers.

FIREARMS: Yes

PETS ON LEASH: Yes

TRAIL INFORMATION

From Lakeside Ranger Station, drive south .2 miles on Highway 260 towards McNary. Turn left on Porter Mountain Road (Forest Road 45) and drive 2.2 miles towards Vernon. Turn left at the cattle guard and drive 75 yards to the cindered trailhead on the right.

The Timber Mesa Trail is one of the many trails included in the White Mountain Trail System in the Lakeside Ranger District.

The 6-mile trail follows along the top edge of the mesa and loops back along the Timber Mesa Fire Road. Hike trail counter clockwise for best results. This is an easy family hike.

TIMBER MESA TRAIL #636

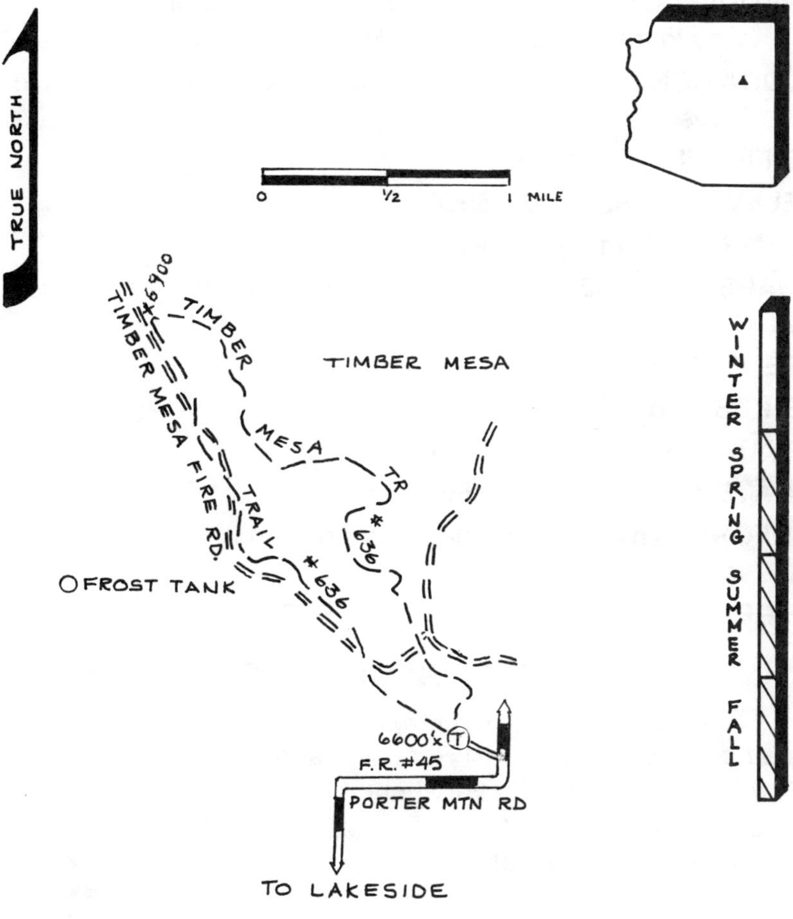

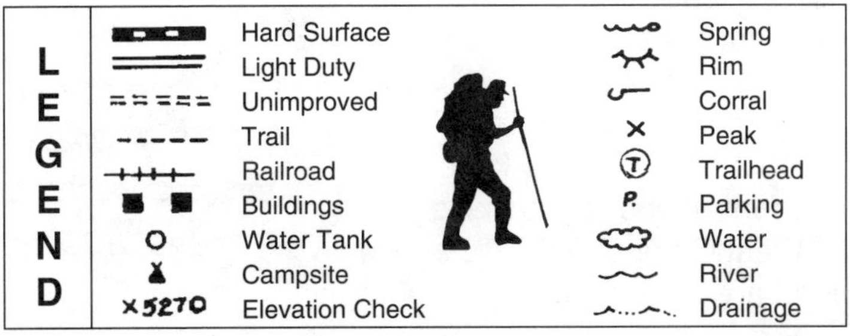

TRAMWAY TRAIL #32

ATTRACTION: Endless varieties of vegetation including wild grapes, views of West Clear Creek, unique geological area.

REQUIREMENTS: Food, water, sturdy boots, proper maps; car okay to trailhead; 3/4 hour hiking time one way.

LOCATION: Long Valley Ranger District - Coconino National Forest.

DIFFICULTY: Difficult

ELEVATIONS: 6700' - 5950'

LENGTH: 3/4 mile one way.

MAPS REQUIRED: U.S.G.S. 7.5 min. topographic for Calloway Butte.

PERMIT: No

BIKES: No

EQUESTRIAN: Not suitable.

WATER: Yes - best to bring your own.

INFORMATION: Watch closely for poison ivy; also, this is bear country.

FIREARMS: Yes **PETS ON LEASH:** Yes

TRAIL INFORMATION

Take Lake Mary Road (FH 3) 7 miles north of Clint's Well, make a left turn (west) on Forest Road #81 and follow to the junction of Forest Road #81E. Travel about 4 miles on Forest Road #81E to Forest Road #693, at the end of which is the trailhead.

As you leave the parking area, the trail starts its descent into the canyon. Watch for fantastic views around you. You are in for a wide variety of vegetation, wildlife and geologic formations as you make your way to West Clear Creek. It's a nice secluded area.

TRAMWAY TRAIL #32

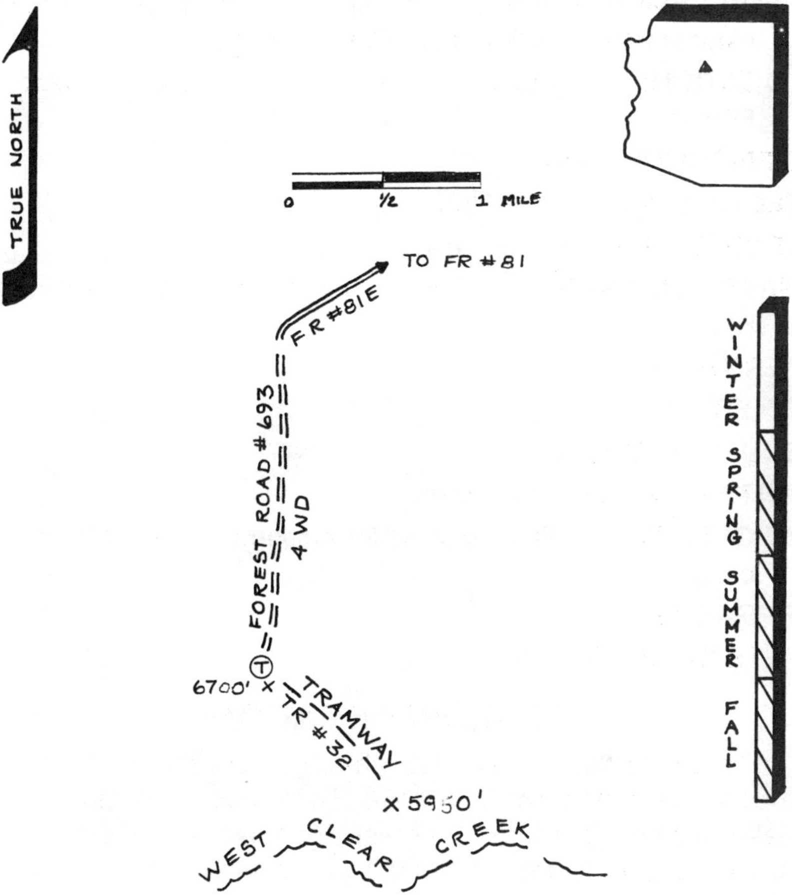

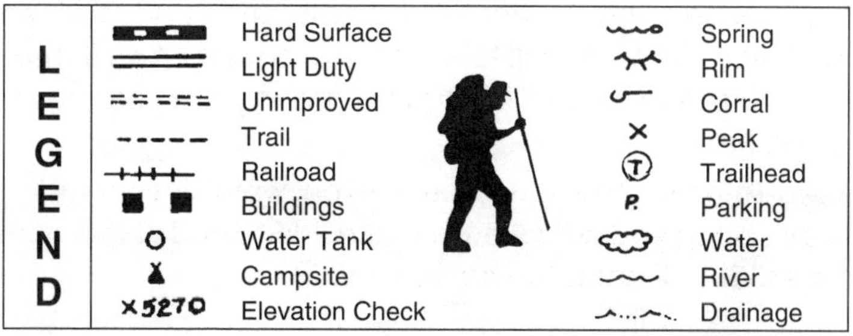

WILLOW CROSSING TRAIL #38

ATTRACTION: Very shaded, endless varieties of vegetation, including wild grapes.

REQUIREMENTS: Food, water, sturdy boots, proper maps; car okay to trailhead; 3/4 hour hiking time one way.

LOCATION: Long Valley Ranger District - Coconino National Forest.

DIFFICULTY: Easy

ELEVATIONS: 6720' - 6800'

LENGTH: 1.3 miles one way.

MAPS REQUIRED: U.S.G.S. 7.5 min. topographic for Calloway Butte.

PERMIT: No

BIKES: No

EQUESTRIAN: Yes

WATER: No - bring your own.

INFORMATION: Watch closely for poison ivy; also, this is bear country.

FIREARMS: Yes

PETS ON LEASH: Yes

TRAIL INFORMATION

Take Lake Mary Road (FH 3) about 4 miles north of Clint's Well and turn west on Forest Road #196. Travel about 2 miles and then make another right turn on Forest Road #122A. After passing through a gate at Peck's Point Tank (close gate behind you), continue to road's end and trailhead.

Trail will head northwest as you enter the very upper area of Willow Valley. The trail will follow minor tributaries as it makes its way and then drops into Willow Valley, giving you a chance to study the varied habitat.

As you start to climb out of the canyon, watch for cairns to guide your way. Soon you will follow a fence line to end of trail at Forest Road #9366M. Return the same way.

WILLOW CROSSING TRAIL #38

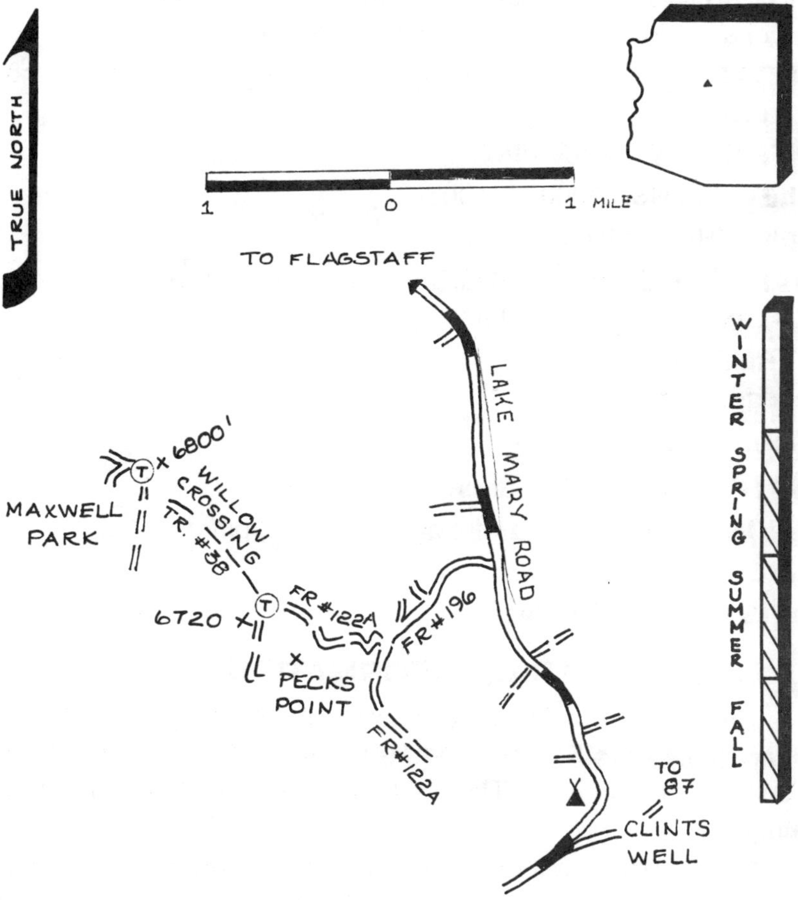

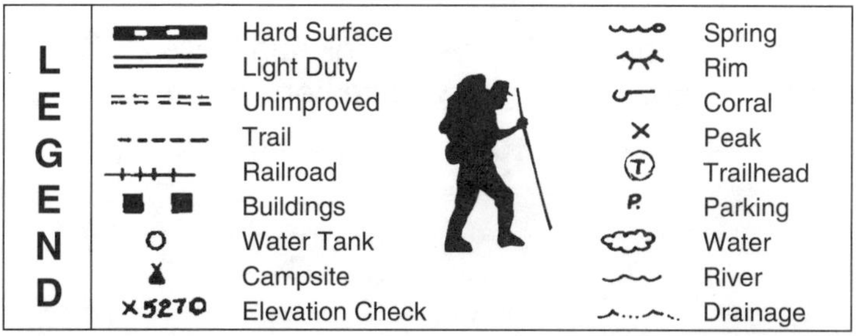

LAKE VIEW TRAIL #132

ATTRACTION: Fantastic views of Mormon Lake and volcanic hillsides.

REQUIREMENTS: Food, water, sturdy boots, proper maps; car okay to trailhead; 1 hour hiking time one way.

LOCATION: Mormon Lake Ranger District, north of Mormon Lake.

DIFFICULTY: Moderate

ELEVATIONS: 7200' - 7400'

LENGTH: 2 miles one way.

MAPS REQUIRED: U.S.G.S. 7.5 min. topographic for Mormon Lake-Mormon Mountain.

PERMIT: No

BIKES: No

EQUESTRIAN: Yes

WATER: No - bring your own

INFORMATION: Be careful of rock outcroppings.

FIREARMS: Yes

PETS ON LEASH: Yes

TRAIL INFORMATION

Take Lake Mary Road 20 miles south from Flagstaff to Forest Road #90. Take Forest Road #90 west for 4.6 miles to Double Springs Campground. The trailhead is at the south side of the campground.

About midway will be a very obvious rock outcropping where you will want to spend some time. This is a perfect picture-taking spot with endless panorama.

The trail continues to Windsor Tank and trail's end at a green mountain meadow. Watch for wildlife here.

LAKE VIEW TRAIL #132

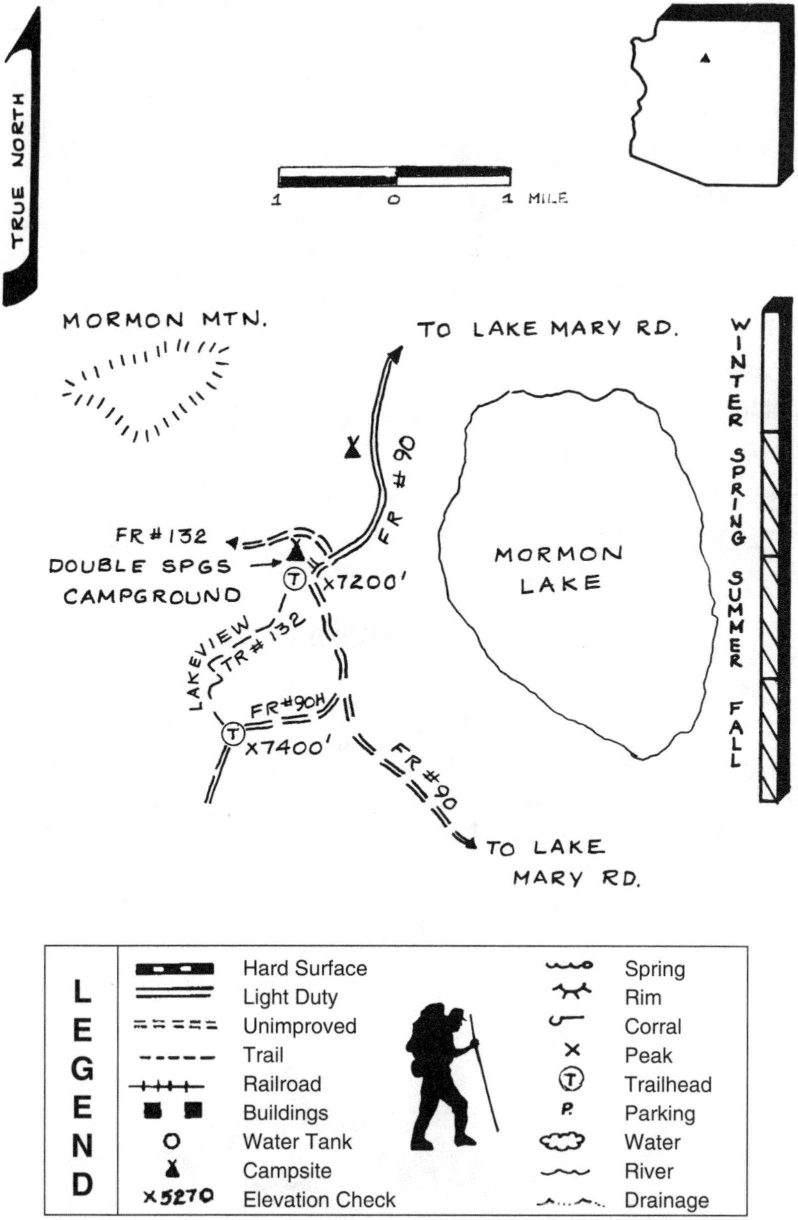

MORMON MOUNTAIN TRAIL #58

ATTRACTION: Numerous fine views; view of Mormon Lake is great as well as the San Francisco Peaks.

REQUIREMENTS: Food, water, sturdy boots, proper maps; car okay to trailhead; 5 hours hiking time round trip.

LOCATION: Mormon Lake Ranger District - Mormon Mountain.

DIFFICULTY: Moderate

ELEVATIONS: 6950' - 8449'

LENGTH: 3 miles one way.

MAPS REQUIRED: U.S.G.S. 7.5 min. topographic for Mormon Lake-Mormon Mountain.

PERMIT: No

BIKES: No

EQUESTRIAN: Yes

WATER: No - bring your own.

INFORMATION: No motorized vehicles.

FIREARMS: Yes

PETS ON LEASH: Yes

TRAIL INFORMATION

Drive south from Flagstaff on Lake Mary Road for 20 miles and turn west at the Forest Road #90 intersection. Continue 3.5 miles to the Montezuma Lodge turnoff, and drive .6 mile on a dirt road to the trailhead.

The trail begins from the rear of Dairy Springs Campground, just west of the road that borders Mormon Lake's western shore. The trail shares a nature trail for awhile, but soon will strike out on its own for its abrupt climb to the summit of Mormon Mountain.

Shortly before the top, you will join an old road to the end of the trail.

MORMON MOUNTAIN TRAIL #58

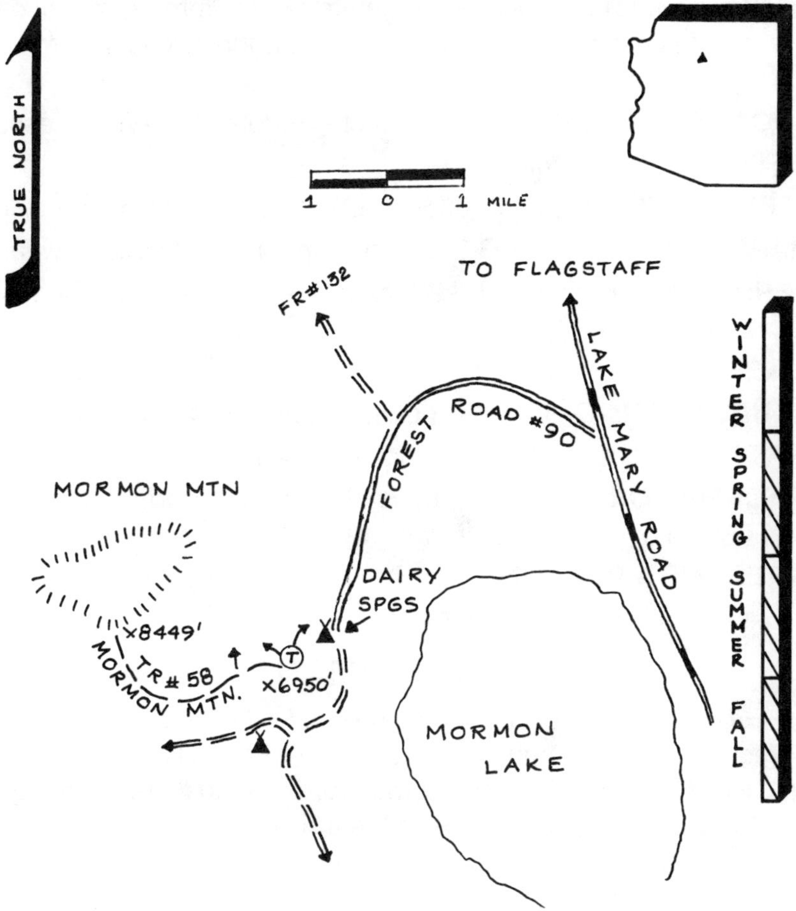

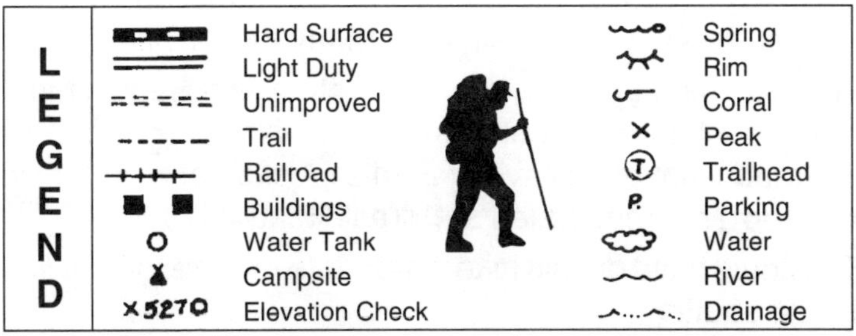

NANKOWEAP TRAIL #57

ATTRACTION: Great views around and into Marble Canyon, very remote area.

REQUIREMENTS: Food, water, sturdy boots, proper maps; car okay to trailhead in dry conditions; 4.5 hours hiking time round trip.

LOCATION: Kaibab Ranger District - Saddle Mtn. Wilderness.

DIFFICULTY: Difficult

ELEVATIONS: 8800' - 6600' **LENGTH:** 12 miles round trip.

MAPS REQUIRED: U.S.G.S. 7.5 min. topographic for Nankoweap.

PERMIT: No - Kaibab Forest Service Area; Yes - Grand Canyon National Park.

BIKES: No

EQUESTRIAN: Only well-experienced horses and riders.

WATER: Not dependable - bring your own.

INFORMATION: Highway #67 is closed after the first snowfall. Beware of these roads in wet weather.

FIREARMS & PETS ON LEASH: Yes, Forest Service Area. No, Grand Canyon National Park.

TRAIL INFORMATION

From the Kaibab Visitor's Center, take Highway 67 south to Forest Road #611 (about 27 miles). Follow Forest Road #611 east just under 2 miles to its junction with Forest Road #610. Turn right (south) and continue 13 miles to the trailhead.

Trail will head due east and, in just over 1 mile, the Grand Canyon National Park Nankcweap Trail heads into Grand Canyon National Park (permit required). At this junction, stay left to continue on Nankoweap Trail #57. Many nice views are await.

At about the 3-mile mark is the junction with Saddle Mountain Trail #31, which travels east from here to within 1 mile of the edge of the Grand Canyon. Stay left at this junction and, in 1 mile, the Nankoweap Trail terminates at Forest Road #445.

You could build on this hike via Saddle Mountain Trail #31 and a possible shuttle.

NANKOWEAP TRAIL #57

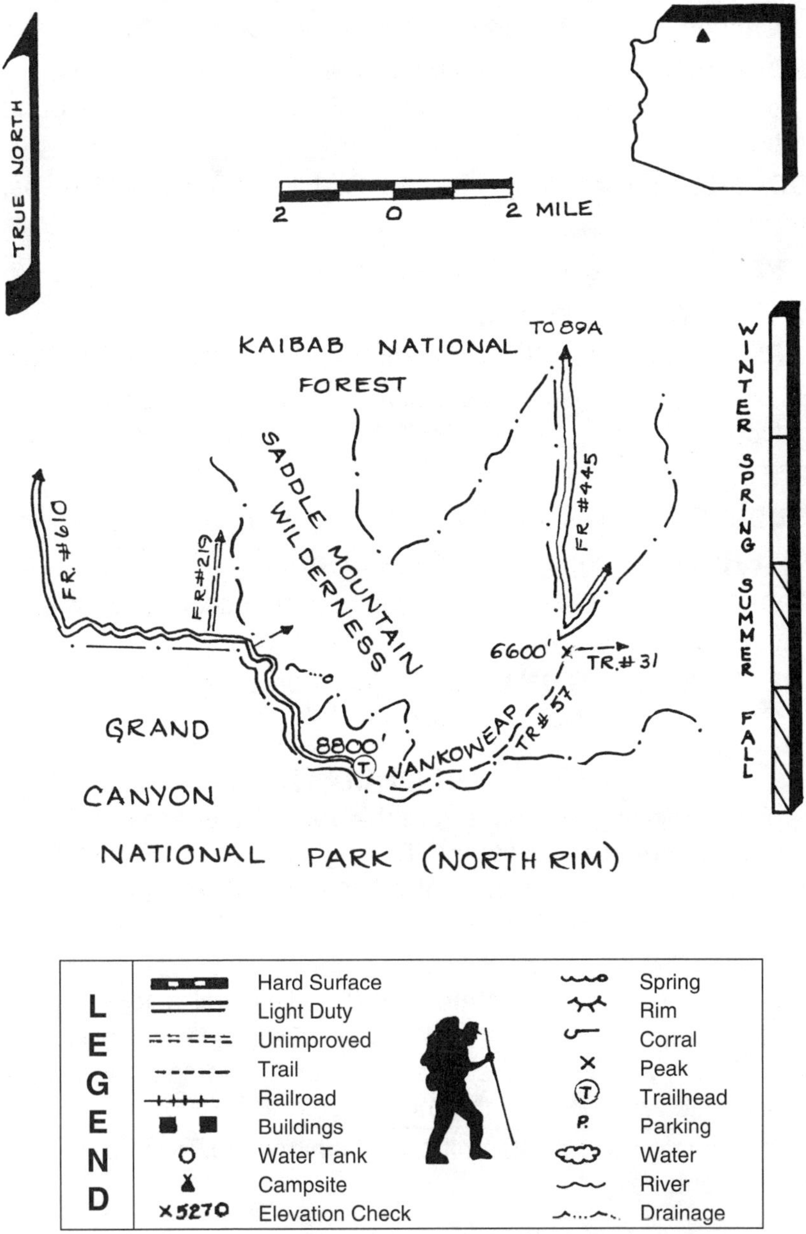

SADDLE MOUNTAIN TRAIL #31

ATTRACTION: Trail ends about 1 mile from the edge of Grand Canyon, but a short cross-country hike takes you there.

REQUIREMENTS: Food, water, sturdy boots, proper maps; car okay to trailhead in dry conditions; 5.5 hours hiking time round trip.

LOCATION: Kaibab Ranger District - Saddle Mountain Wilderness.

DIFFICULTY: Easy

ELEVATIONS: 6600' - 7100' - 6600'

LENGTH: 6 miles one way.

MAPS REQUIRED: U.S.G.S. 7.5 min. topographic for Nankoweap.

PERMIT: No - Kaibab Forest Service Area; Yes - Grand Canyon National Park.

BIKES: No

EQUESTRIAN: Yes

WATER: Not dependable - bring your own.

INFORMATION: Can be hot in summer; trail access roads less than ideal when wet.

FIREARMS & PETS ON LEASH: Yes - Forest Service Area. No, Grand Canyon National Park.

TRAIL INFORMATION

Take Highway 89A east from the Jacob Lake area to Forest Road #445 (about 19-20 miles). Turn right (south) on Forest Road #445 and stay on its right fork all the way to the trailhead of Nankoweap Trail #57 (just under 28 miles), and park here.

You will travel on about 1 mile of Nankoweap Trail #57 to the actual start of Saddle Mountain Trail #31. This trail is, for the most part, level from here to the end. You will have great views of House Rock Valley, and I would suggest a short cross-country hike at trail's end for your view of the mighty Colorado River.

You could build on this hike via Nankoweap Trail #57 and a possible shuttle.

SADDLE MOUNTAIN TRAIL #31

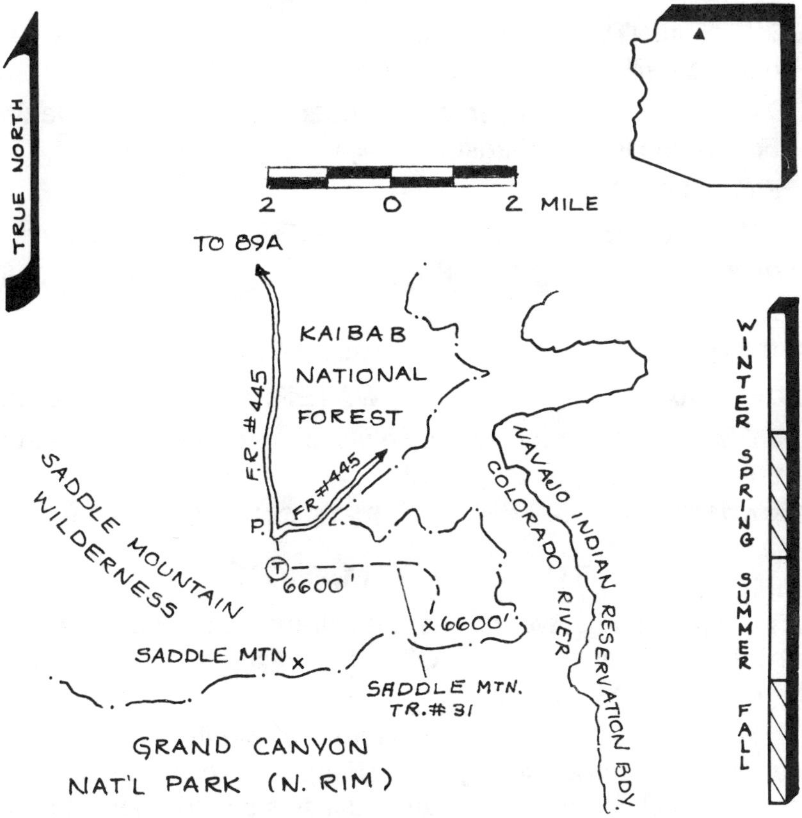

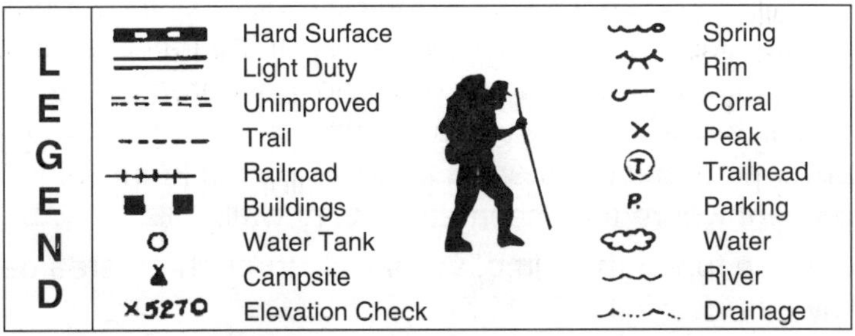

ELDEN LOOKOUT TRAIL #4

ATTRACTION: Elden Lookout Trail connects to Oldham Trail at the top of the mountain making a long loop hike possible, if you park a car at Buffalo Park or arrange a pickup there.

REQUIREMENTS: Water, snack, sturdy boots, proper maps; car okay to trailhead; 2.5 hours hiking time one way.

LOCATION: Peaks Ranger District, near Flagstaff Mall on Santa Fe Avenue in east Flagstaff.

DIFFICULTY: Difficult

ELEVATIONS: 6900' - 9295' **LENGTH:** 3 miles one way.

MAPS REQUIRED: U.S.G.S. 7.5 min. topographic for Flagstaff East.

PERMIT: No **BIKES:** No

EQUESTRIAN: No **WATER:** No - bring your own.

INFORMATION: No motorized vehicles, no horses, because of the trail's extreme steep grade.

FIREARMS: Yes **PETS ON LEASH:** Yes

TRAIL INFORMATION

Follow Santa Fe Avenue past the entrance to the Flagstaff Mall and the Peaks Ranger District Office to a trailhead parking lot just off the north side of the street.

This trail leads you up a staircase of petrified lava to the mountain's summit 2,300 feet above Flagstaff. The route starts as a gradual climb along the shorter and less steep Fatman's Loop, but increases in gradient as the Lookout Trail strikes out on its own ascent to the mountain top. Along the way, you'll want to stop and catch your breath while you enjoy breathtaking views of the city and surrounding area, as well as intimate views of the mountain's very visible geology. The lower reaches of the trail pass through a mixed pinyon-juniper woodland and ponderosa pine forest, changing to mixed conifers as you climb. You may be surprised to encounter a couple of different kinds of cactus in this high, cold environment where they seem to do very well.

Near the top of the climb, you'll walk through an area devastated by a huge wildfire in 1977.

ELDEN LOOKOUT TRAIL #4

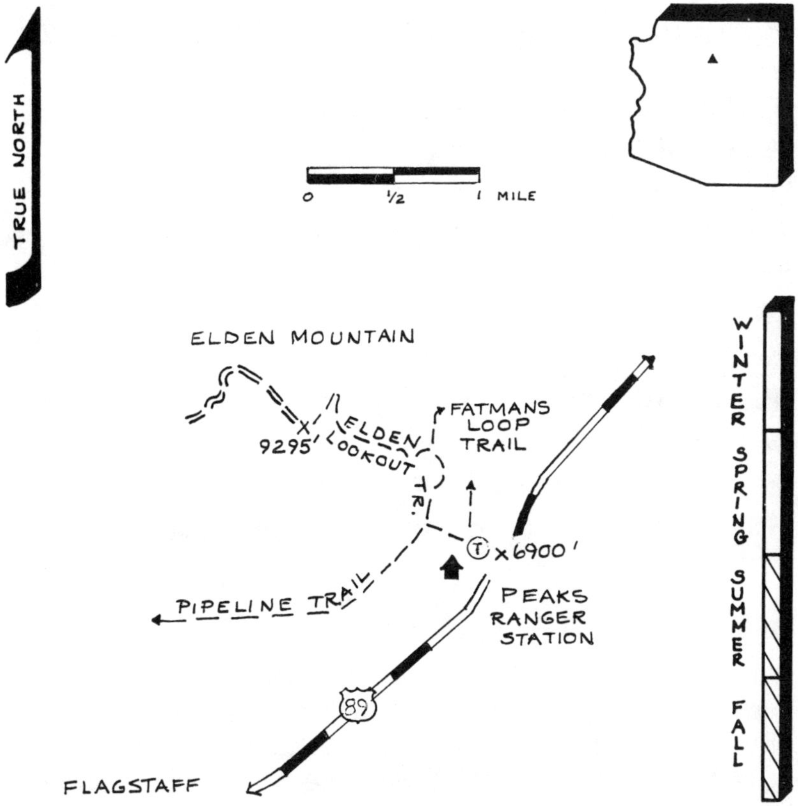

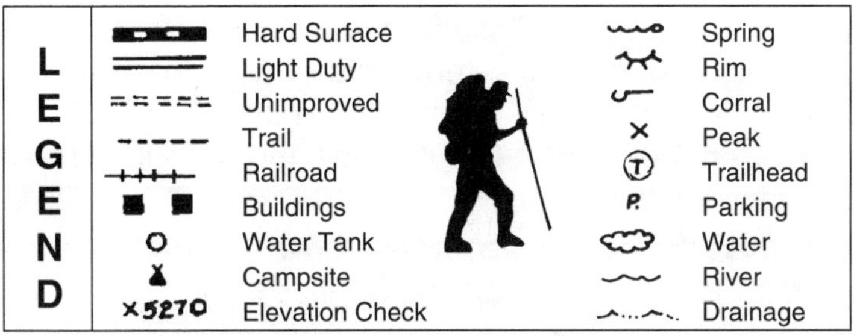

HEART TRAIL #103

ATTRACTION: A close look at a regenerating forest.

REQUIREMENTS: Water, food, sturdy boots, proper maps; car okay to trailhead; 2.5 hours hiking time one way.

LOCATION: Peaks Ranger District, north of Flagstaff on graveled roads.

DIFFICULTY: Difficult

ELEVATIONS: 7200' - 8500'

LENGTH: 3.5 miles one way.

MAPS REQUIRED: U.S.G.S. 7.5 min. topographic for Sunset Crater West.

PERMIT: No

BIKES: Yes, but not recommended.

EQUESTRIAN: Yes

WATER: No - bring your own.

INFORMATION: Not a good trail for a novice.

FIREARMS: Yes

PETS ON LEASH: Yes

TRAIL INFORMATION

The best access to Heart Trail would be to begin at the Sandy Seep trailhead. This is approximately 1.5 miles north of the Peaks Ranger Station on Highway 89, just past Elden Pueblo on the west side of the highway. The trail is within the incorporated boundaries of Flagstaff and can be reached by the Fatman Loop Trail and the Little Elden Trail.

The Heart Trail begins in the Sandy Seep area just north of Flagstaff at approximately 7200 feet, and climbs the east slope of Mt. Elden to connect with Sunset Trail in Sunset Park. As the trail climbs, it winds through the remnants of a large, mixed conifer forest which was destroyed by the Radio Fire in 1977. The area is well into regeneration, with Gamble oak and various grasses and shrubs growing strong.

The Heart Trail can be accessed from a number of trails--Little Elden Trail, Sandy Seep Trail and Sunset Trail.

HEART TRAIL #103

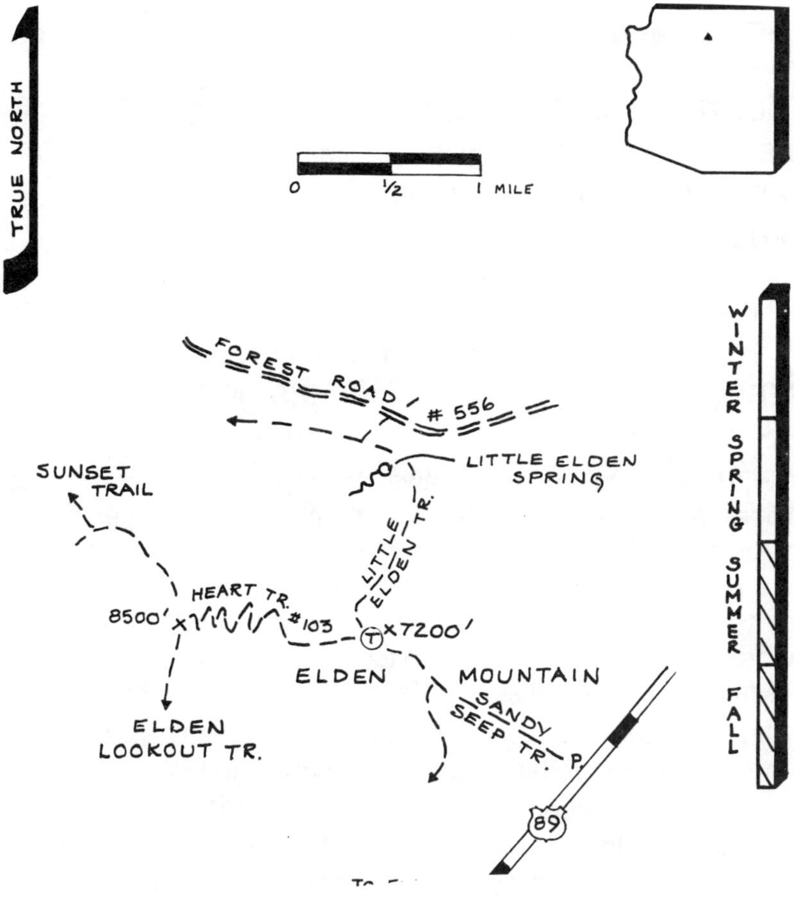

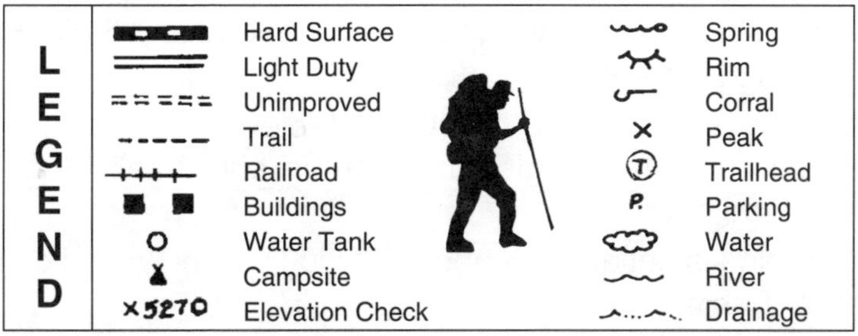

HUMPHREYS PEAK TRAIL #104

ATTRACTION: Here you can stand on the highest real estate in Arizona, as well as the only tundra in the state. After you sign in at the top, relax and see how many points of interest you can identify from your vantage point; they are just endless.

REQUIREMENTS: Food, water, rain gear, map, waterproof shelter; 8 hours round trip.

LOCATION: San Francisco Peaks, Flagstaff, AZ

DIFFICULTY: Difficult; know your limits and obey them.

ELEVATIONS: 9590' - 12,633'

LENGTH: 8.7 miles round trip.

MAPS REQUIRED: Humphreys Peak Quadrangle; 7.5 minute topographic, Coconino County. This trail is not on your map but it should be taken anyway for reference.

PERMIT: No **BIKES:** No

EQUESTRIAN: No **WATER:** Bring your own

INFORMATION: All of the laws and regulations pertaining to a Wilderness apply on the Peaks. The elevation changes as does the steepness of the routes. On the upper slopes, the wind can be severe; winds over 50 miles per hour are common. Pacific cold fronts with accompanying rain or snow can move in very quickly. A forested area *away from* ridge tops, ledges or rock outcrops and the tallest trees is the safest place to be if a storm threatens.

Do not underestimate the thin air on this peak; you would be wise to prepare for this hike by hiking 8000' to 9000' peaks first.

A call to the airport at Flagstaff, 520-774-3301, will give you the latest weather information. Patches of snow may remain into July. Violent electrical storms occur almost daily during July, and frequently during other spring, summer and fall months. Warning—hikers may find their hair standing on end and their clothing aglow with static electricity.

Once you reach the 11,400-foot elevation, you are near timberline. Stunted Englemann spruce and small bristlecone pines can be seen.

Camping is not allowed above 11,000-foot elevation or within the Inner Basin.

HUMPHREYS PEAK TRAIL #104

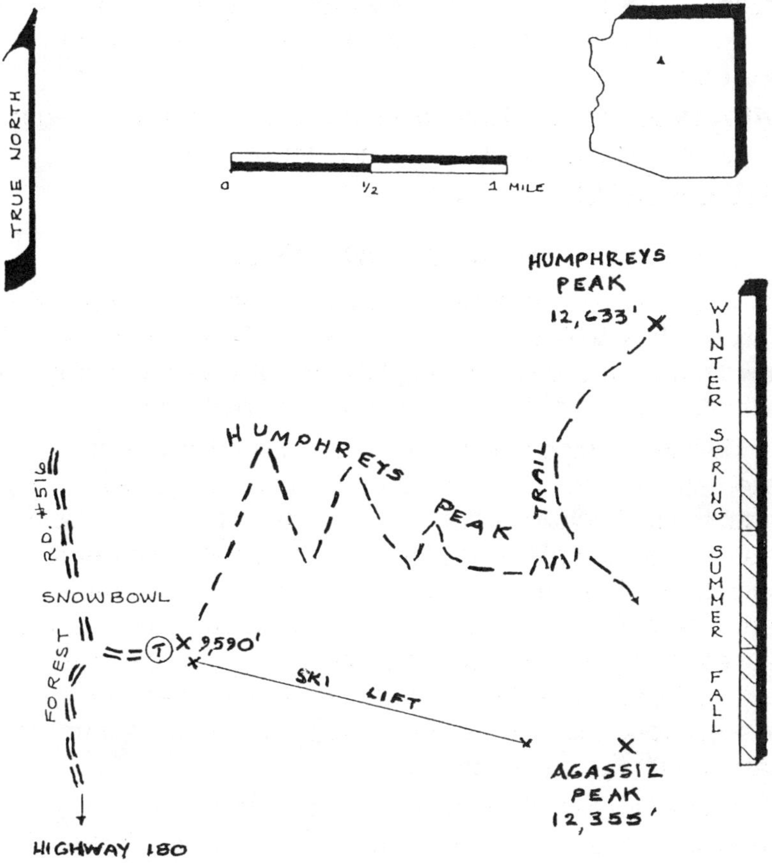

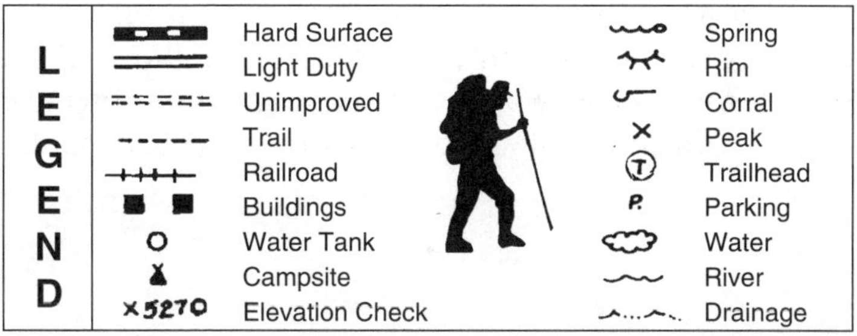

Hiking above timberline is restricted to designated trails only. Indiscriminate cross-country hiking is prohibited.

The San Francisco Peaks' groundsel, scientifically known as *Senecio franciscanus,* is a small plant growing above timberline. It grows nowhere else in the world.

At 12,633 feet, Humphreys Peak is the highest point in Arizona. This small region in the San Francisco Peaks (eroded volcanic cones) is the only place in Arizona where tundra conditions exist.

FIREARMS: Not restricted, but there is absolutely no need for a gun nor its extra weight on a hike this difficult.

PETS ON LEASH: Yes

TRAIL INFORMATION

To get to the trailhead from Flagstaff, drive north on US 180 for 7 miles to F.R. 516, the Snow Bowl Road. Drive 7.4 miles on this paved road to the lower parking lot of the Snow Bowl facility. The trailhead is located at the north end of the parking lot.

This hiking experience cannot be matched by any other in the state. After leaving the parking lot and continuing past the upper lodge, the trail actually parallels the ski tram for a short distance. This is as good a place as any to use discipline in order to pace yourself, which is mandatory on a trail this steep and high. Already steep, the trail now continues away from the ski lift (NE) as it starts a series of long switchbacks, and travels through aspens along the way. As the switchbacks get shorter and the trail steepens, you will have escaped the treeline and windy conditions are sure to be present (50 m.p.h. are common).

When you reach the saddle between Humphreys and Agassiz, you must not, for any reason, hike over to Agassiz Peak; it is off limits. This is a good place to take stock of how you feel before continuing the last mile or so to the Peak (left turn); this last mile requires one solid hour of travel. However, for those of you that make it to the top, the views will be fantastic as you sit on the throne of Arizona. Sign the register and return the way you came. Consult your map.

A late fall hike on the Kachina Trail.
(Photo by Christine M. Hamel)

Ice sculptures formed by the wind—Humphreys Peak.
(Photo by John Villinski)

Fall aspens on the Kachina Trail.
(Photo by Christine M. Hamel)

KACHINA TRAIL #150

ATTRACTION: Fantastic views; abundant wildlife.

REQUIREMENTS: Water, food, sturdy boots, proper maps; car okay to trailheads; 2.5 hours hiking time one way.

LOCATION: Peaks Ranger District, 17 miles north of Flagstaff on paved highways and gravel forest roads.

DIFFICULTY: Moderate **ELEVATIONS:** 9600' - 9850' - 8780'

LENGTH: 5 miles one way.

MAPS REQUIRED: U.S.G.S. 7.5 min. topographic for Humphrey's Peak.

PERMIT: No **BIKES:** No

EQUESTRIAN: Yes **WATER:** No - bring your own.

INFORMATION: Bring a jacket as it can be cool at these altitudes.

FIREARMS: Yes **PETS ON LEASH:** No

TRAIL INFORMATION

Drive 7 miles northwest of Flagstaff on US 180 and turn north (right) onto the Snow Bowl Road (Forest Road 516). Follow this paved road about 7 miles to the Snow Bowl Ski Area. Drive into the first parking lot on the right (south). The Kachina trailhead is located at the south end of the parking lot.

Most trails on the San Francisco Peaks head right for the top of this extinct volcano, the tallest mountain in the state of Arizona. The Kachina Trail breaks this pattern by setting an easy course across some of the mountain's more moderate topography. Don't let that discourage you if you think maximum altitude provides maximum enjoyment. This friendly pathway provides access to a healthy portion of the mountain's most beautiful scenery. Its gently rolling course winds along the mountain's middle slopes almost entirely within the boundaries of the Kachina Peaks Wilderness Area. It follows a moderate gradient through stands of white-barked aspen and groves of tall, mixed conifers separated by broad, wildflower-carpeted meadows. At a number of points, the trail breaks free of the trees to offer good views, both of the rocky upper slopes of the mountain and of the forests surrounding its base. Portions of the city of Flagstaff are visible as well.

KACHINA TRAIL #150

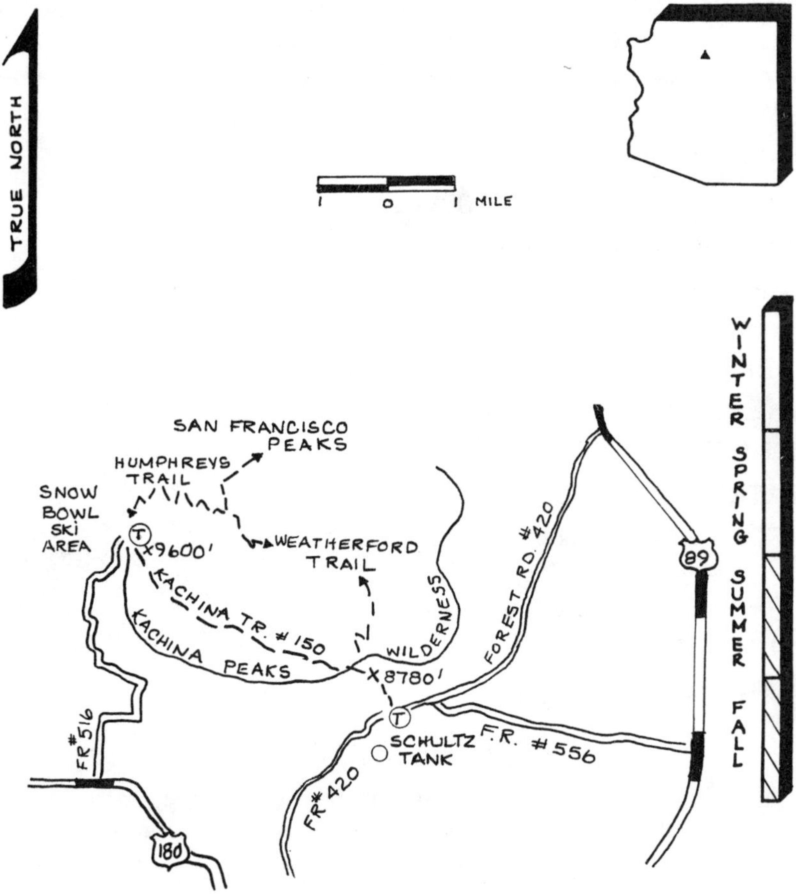

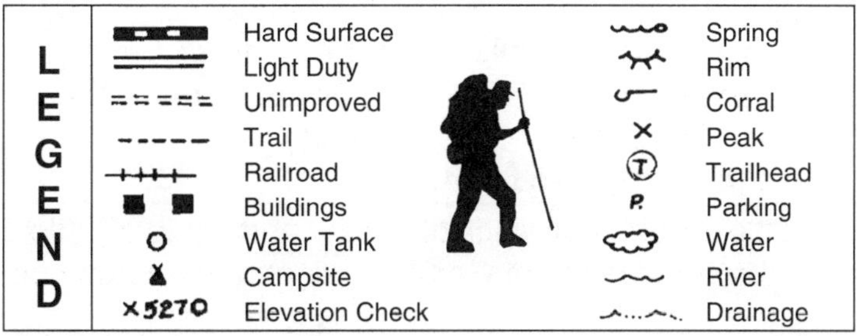

LITTLE ELDEN TRAIL

ATTRACTION: Easy access and ease of travel for some great scenery.

REQUIREMENTS: Water, food, sturdy boots, proper maps; car okay to trailhead; 2.5 hours hiking time one way.

LOCATION: Peaks Ranger District, 3 miles north of Flagstaff off U.S. 89.

DIFFICULTY: Easy

ELEVATIONS: 7200' - 7800'

LENGTH: 4.7 miles one way.

MAPS REQUIRED: U.S.G.S. 7.5 min. topographic for Sunset Crater West.

PERMIT: No

BIKES: Yes

EQUESTRIAN: Yes

WATER: No - bring your own.

INFORMATION: This trail may also be accessed from Schultz Tank or via the Sandy Seep Trail.

FIREARMS: Yes

PETS ON LEASH: Yes

TRAIL INFORMATION

Drive 5 miles northeast of Flagstaff on U.S. 89. Turn west (left) on Forest Road 556 and drive 2 miles to Little Elden trailhead located on the south (left) side of the road across from Forest Road 556A.

Little Elden Trail begins within the boundaries of the city of Flagstaff, then leads the hiker into the heart of the Peaks trail system, at Schultz Tank. From this point you can connect to the Dry Lake Hills/Mt. Elden trails to the south, or the Kachina Peaks Wilderness trail system to the north.

The Little Elden Trail winds along the north side of Little Elden Mountain through stands of Gamble oak and ponderosa pine.

LITTLE ELDEN TRAIL

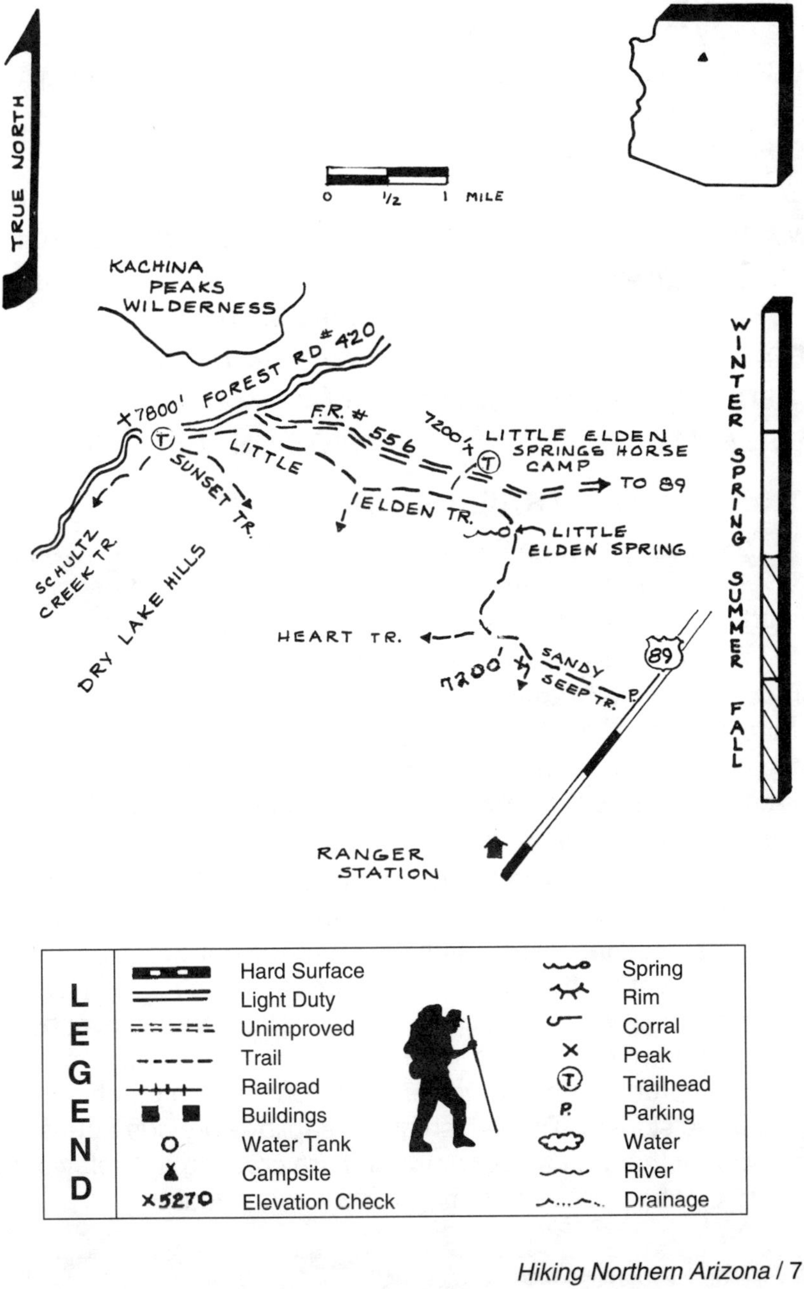

SANDY SEEP TRAIL #129

ATTRACTION: Abundant wildlife; nice family trail; a chance to see a regenerating forest up close.

REQUIREMENTS: Water, snack, sturdy boots, proper maps; car okay to trailhead; 1.5 hours round trip.

LOCATION: Peaks Ranger District, on east side of Flagstaff, within city limits.

DIFFICULTY: Moderate

ELEVATIONS: 6850' - 7200'

LENGTH: 1.5 miles one way.

MAPS REQUIRED: U.S.G.S. 7.5 min. topographic for Sunset Crater West and Flagstaff East.

PERMIT: No

BIKES: Yes

EQUESTRIAN: Yes

WATER: No - bring your own.

INFORMATION: No motorized entry of any kind.

FIREARMS: Yes

PETS ON LEASH: Yes

TRAIL INFORMATION

Drive east through Flagstaff on U.S. 89A (Santa Fe Avenue). One half mile beyond the Townsend/Winona Road intersection, a short Forest Road (9139) turns west to the trailhead.

The Sandy Seep area on the eastern slopes of Mt. Elden is an important winter range for mule deer, as well as a valuable recreation resource for the Flagstaff area. The trail that provides access to it follows an old jeep track that meanders through the open grasslands dotted with ponderosa pines, Gamble oaks and clumps of cliff rose.

Mt. Elden is covered with dead trees killed by the disastrous Radio Fire of 1977. Climbing higher you'll see evidence of the fire closer at hand, including numbers of burned out snags as well as the remains of old fire breaks plowed into the landscape. Near the end of the trail, you'll be hiking on land that was burned over by the fire and get a close look at how the area is naturally regenerating. Pioneer sprouts of oak at lower elevations and aspen higher up carpet the slopes. These lush green saplings provide nourishing browse for the area's deer herd, and are creating a display of fall colors that becomes more magnificent every year.

SANDY SEEP TRAIL #129

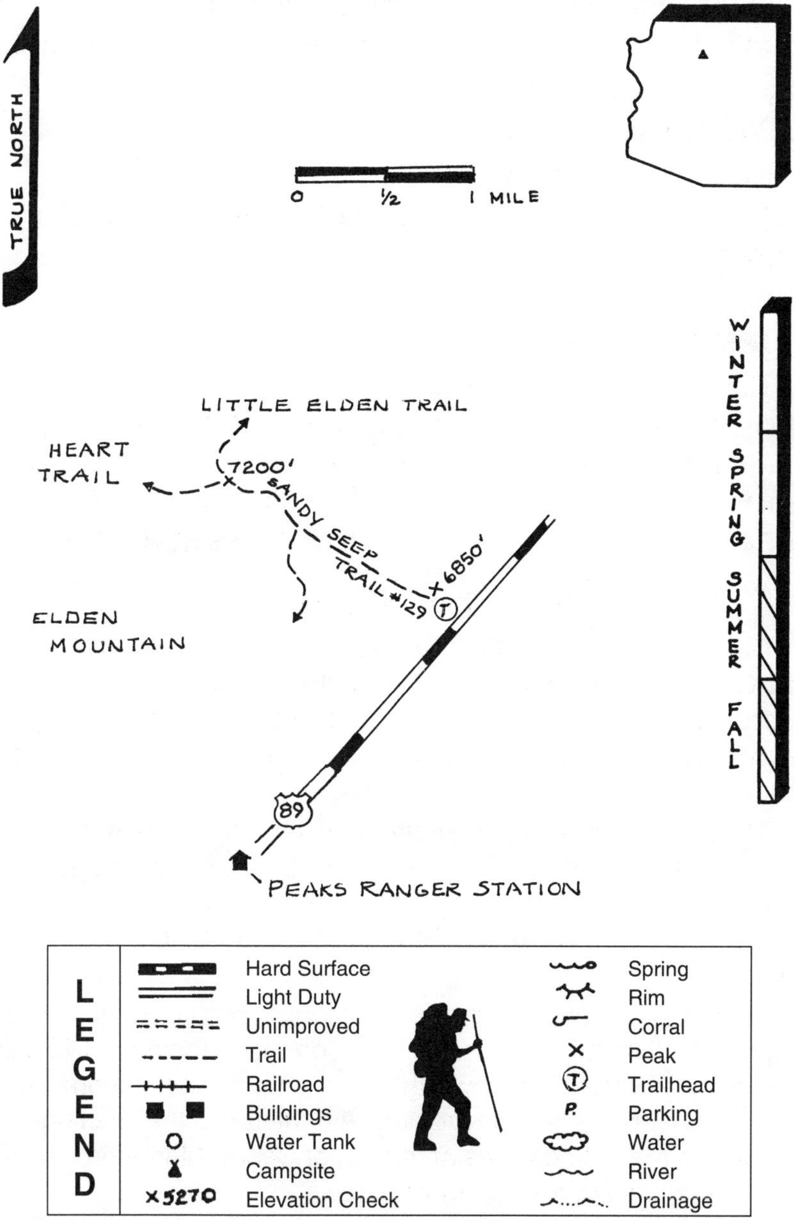

LOY TRAIL #5

ATTRACTION: Very scenic.

REQUIREMENTS: Food, water, sturdy boots, proper maps; car okay to trailhead; 4.5 hours hiking time round trip.

LOCATION: Sedona Ranger District, 20 miles west of Sedona.

DIFFICULTY: Moderate to Difficult

ELEVATIONS: 4720' - 6400'

LENGTH: 5 miles one way.

MAPS REQUIRED: U.S.G.S. 7.5 min. topographic for Loy Butte.

PERMIT: No

BIKES: No

EQUESTRIAN: Yes

WATER: No - bring your own.

INFORMATION: The Samuel Loy family moved here in the 1880s to escape the outbreak of malaria along the Verde River at the time. This area is very hot and dry in the summer.

FIREARMS: Yes **PETS ON LEASH:** Yes

TRAIL INFORMATION

Drive 10.7 miles west of Sedona on Hwy 89A, turn right onto Red Canyon Road #525 and follow the signs about 9.3 miles towards Loy Butte. Trailhead will be on your right just before you reach a cattle guard and fence, the boundary of the Hancock Ranch.

The trail follows along the bottom of Loy Canyon for most of its length. The first 4 miles are easy going along this drainage with only a gradual rise in elevation. The last mile at the end of the canyon rises abruptly to a saddle which ties Secret Mountain to the Rim.

Loy Trail junctions with the Secret Mountain Trail at this saddle. By turning left at the junction you will soon reach the end of Forest Road #538. If you follow Loy Trail straight from the junction, it will end shortly with lots of brush cutting. A right turn at the junction will treat you to many fine views at the top of Secret Mountain. Keep an eye on the time; it's a long way down!

LOY TRAIL #5

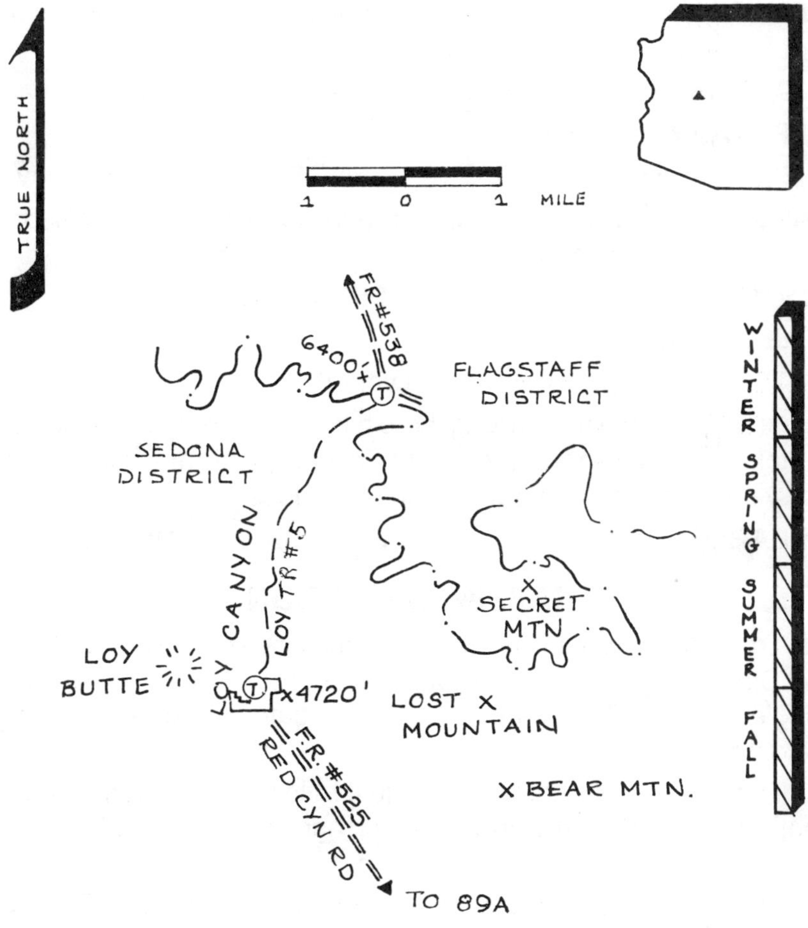
TRUE NORTH
1 0 1 MILE
FR #538
6400'+
FLAGSTAFF
DISTRICT
SEDONA
DISTRICT
LOY CANYON
LOY TR #5
LOY
BUTTE
x4720'
LOST X
MOUNTAIN
X
SECRET
MTN
X BEAR MTN.
F.R. #525
RED CYN RD
TO 89A
WINTER
SPRING
SUMMER
FALL

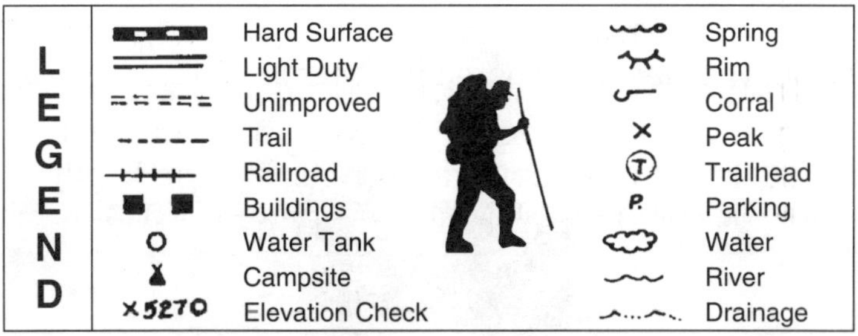
LEGEND
Hard Surface
Light Duty
Unimproved
Trail
Railroad
Buildings
Water Tank
Campsite
x5270 Elevation Check
Spring
Rim
Corral
Peak
Trailhead
P. Parking
Water
River
Drainage

WILSON MOUNTAIN TRAIL #10

ATTRACTION: Views from summit of Oak Creek Canyon: Sedona, Dry Creek Basin, Verde Valley.

REQUIREMENTS: Food, water, sturdy boots, proper maps; car okay to trailhead; 6 hours hiking time round trip.

LOCATION: Sedona Ranger District, north of Sedona.

DIFFICULTY: Difficult

ELEVATIONS: 4600' - 6900' **LENGTH:** 5.6 miles one way.

MAPS REQUIRED: U.S.G.S. 7.5 min. topographic for Wilson Mountain/Munds Park.

PERMIT: No **BIKES:** No

EQUESTRIAN: Yes

WATER: Not dependable - bring your own.

INFORMATION: This is a long, hard hike so start early. One could take North Wilson Trail down to Encinos picnic area with a car shuttle. Watch for bear at higher altitudes.

FIREARMS: Yes **PETS ON LEASH:** Yes

TRAIL INFORMATION

Trail begins about 2 miles north of the intersection of U.S. 89A and State Highway 179 north of Sedona. Park at the east end of Midgley Bridge. Trail starts just past the gate on the east side of the old road.

There is a short, steep stretch just below the first bench, and another similar stretch from the second bench to the summit. Even with all the shade it can be a hot hike.

At the first bench is the intersection of North Wilson Trail, a possible alternate return trip with the use of a car shuttle.

Wilson Mountain and Wilson Canyon were named after Richard Wilson who was killed here by a bear in 1885.

WILSON MOUNTAIN TRAIL #10

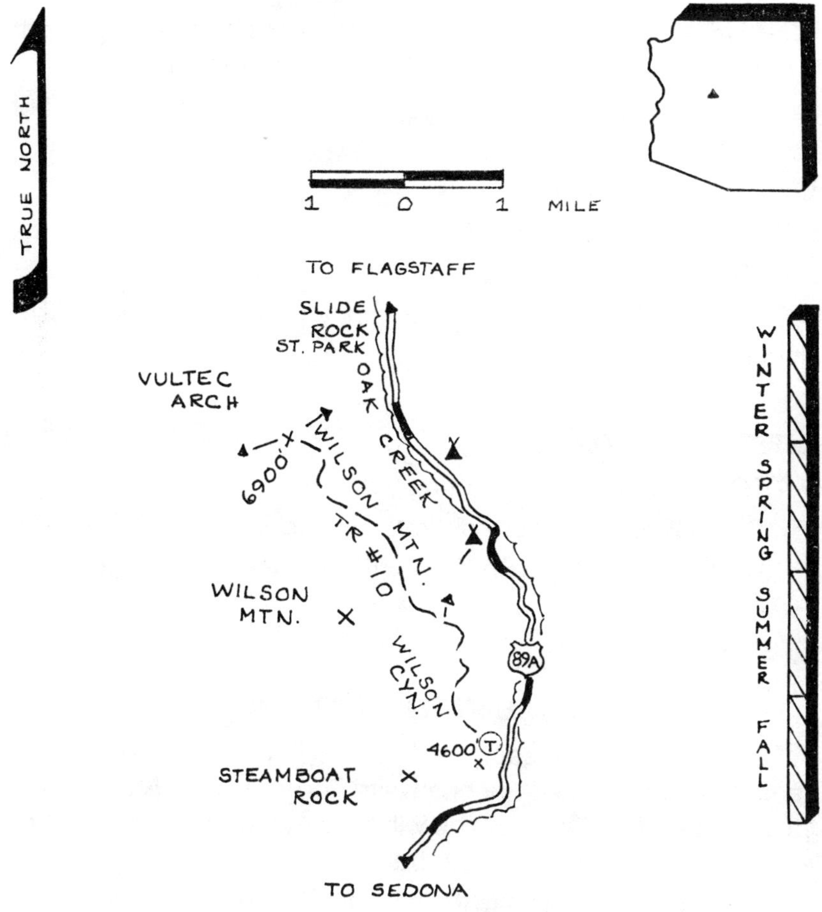

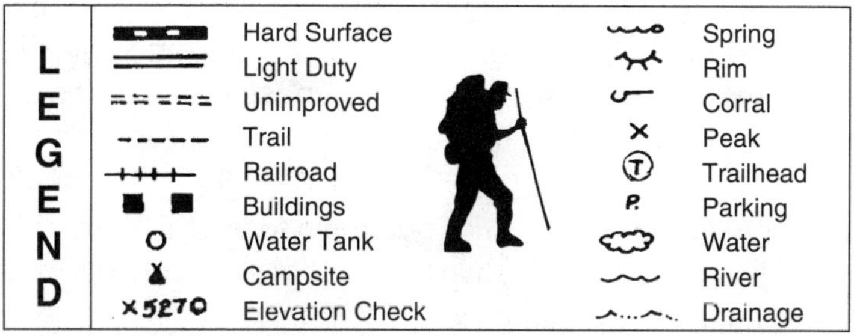

EAST FORK TRAIL #95

ATTRACTION: Fantastic views and breathtaking Alpine environment.

REQUIREMENTS: Food, water, sturdy boots, proper maps; car okay to trailhead; 6-7 hours hiking time round trip.

LOCATION: Springerville Ranger District, 12 miles southeast of Greer.

DIFFICULTY: Moderate

ELEVATIONS: 9150' - 11,000'

LENGTH: 7 miles one way.

MAPS REQUIRED: U.S.G.S. 7.5 min. topographic for Mt. Ord.

PERMIT: No

BIKES: No

EQUESTRIAN: Yes

WATER: Not dependable - bring your own.

INFORMATION: Do not continue on the last 403 feet to the summit—it is sacred Apache land.

FIREARMS: Yes

PETS ON LEASH: Yes

TRAIL INFORMATION

To reach the trailhead, take Forest Road #87 south out of Greer about 6 miles to its junction with Forest Road #113, turn left and continue for 6.2 miles. You will pass the turnoff to Lee Valley Reservoir before arriving at the trailhead, both on the right side.

About 1/2 to 3/4 mile into the hike, the remains of Phelps cabin is on your left. At first you will skirt the east fork of the Little Colorado River. It is not far after the cabin before you enter wilderness area and then the forest. About halfway you will begin some switchbacks. At the 3/4 mark you will leave the wilderness for a short distance, only to return again and complete the hike at the junction of West Fork Trail. Please respect the Off Limits areas on the peak.

You could take West Fork Trail down to its trailhead at Sheep Crossing, but remember the two trailheads are about 4 miles apart. A car shuttle is an excellent plan.

EAST FORK TRAIL #95

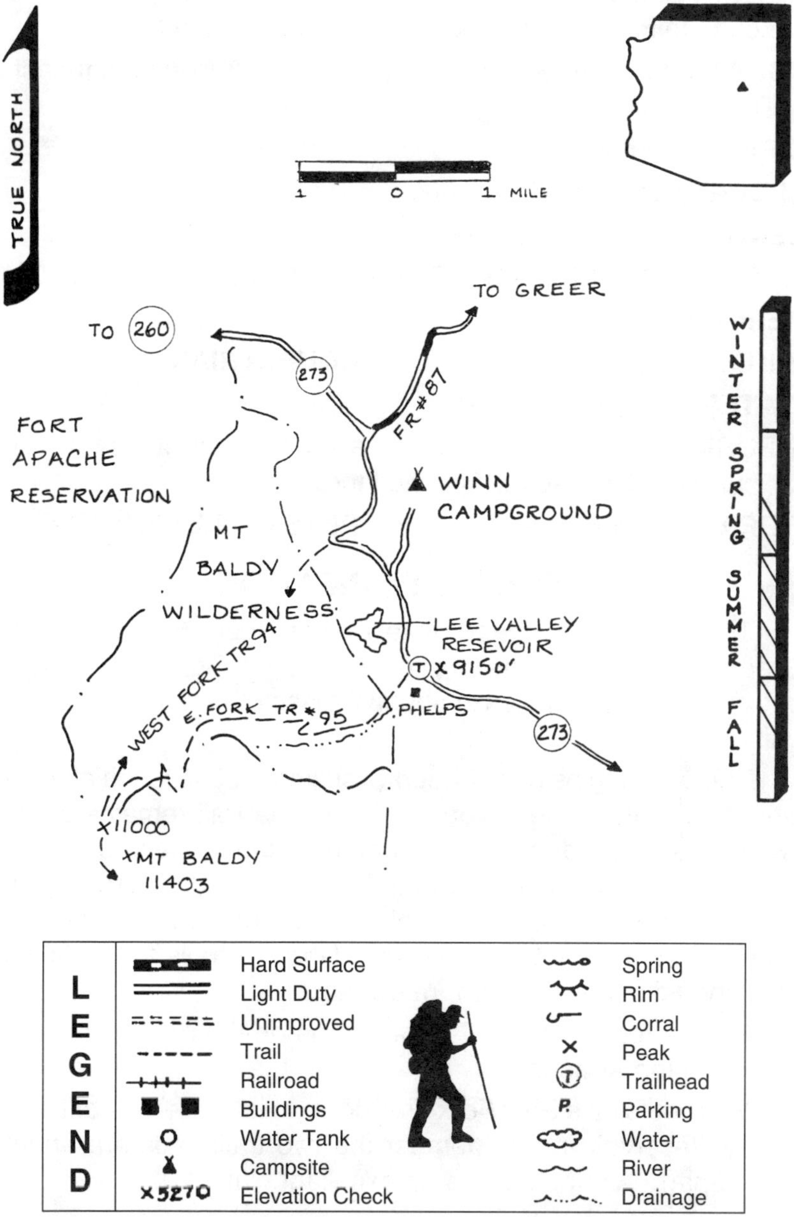

WEST FORK TRAIL #94

ATTRACTION: Fantastic views and breathtaking Alpine environment.

REQUIREMENTS: Food, water, sturdy boots, proper maps; car okay to trailhead; 6-7 hours hiking time round trip.

LOCATION: Springerville Ranger District, 8 miles southeast of Greer.

DIFFICULTY: Moderate

ELEVATIONS: 9200' - 11,000'

LENGTH: 7 miles one way.

MAPS REQUIRED: U.S.G.S. 7.5 min. topographic for Mt. Ord.

PERMIT: No

BIKES: No **EQUESTRIAN:** Yes

WATER: Not dependable.

INFORMATION: Do not continue on the last 403 feet to the summit—it is sacred Apache land.

FIREARMS: Yes **PETS ON LEASH:** Yes

TRAIL INFORMATION

To reach the trailhead, take Forest Road #87 south out of Greer about 6 miles to its junction with Forest Road #113, turn left and continue for 2.2 miles to Sheep Crossing Campground and the trailhead.

This trail begins near Sheep Crossing and ascends along the west fork of the Little Colorado River. The trail remains on soft, grassy slopes for about 2 miles before entering the forest. About 5 miles from the trailhead, you will come to a ridge leading to the top; it is unmistakable as you look down both sides. In another 1.5 miles, you will come to the junction of the two trails at 11,000 feet. This should serve as your turnaround point.

Please respect the Off Limits areas on the peak. These are sacred to the Apaches.

You could take East Fork Trail down to its trailhead east of Lee Valley Reservoir, but remember the two trailheads are about 4 miles apart. A car shuttle is an excellant plan.

WEST FORK TRAIL #94

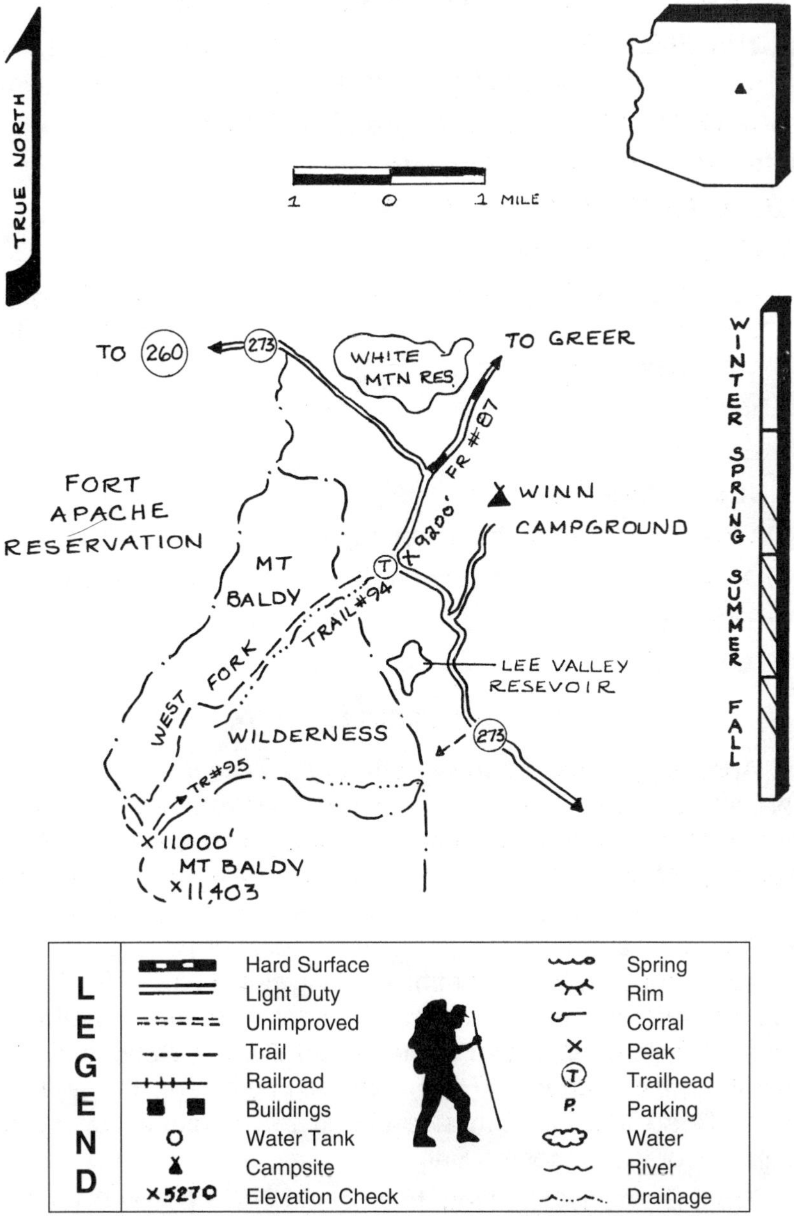

ARIZONA TRAIL
COCONINO RIM SEGMENT

ATTRACTION: Views of Grand Canyon and Painted Desert from old fire tower built in 1936 - climb tower at your own risk.

REQUIREMENTS: Lots of water, food, sturdy boots, proper maps, rain gear; car okay to trailhead; 4 hours hiking time one way.

LOCATION: 10 miles west of Grand Canyon Airport.

DIFFICULTY: Easy to Moderate

ELEVATIONS: 7490' - 7070'

LENGTH: 9.1 miles one way.

MAPS REQUIRED: Kaibab National Forest map (Williams, Chalender, Tusayan Ranger District); Grandview Point quad 15' series - 7.5' series.

PERMIT: No

BIKES: Yes

EQUESTRIAN: Yes

WATER: Not reliable - bring your own.

INFORMATION: Do not camp within 1/4 mile of Russell Tank.

FIREARMS: Yes

PETS ON LEASH: Yes

TRAIL INFORMATION

Access #1: From Highway 64/180 at Tusayan, turn east on Forest Road 302 (.8 mile north of Grand Canyon Airport). Follow the signs for 16 miles to Grandview Lookout Tower. Access #2: Via Highway 64 in Grand Canyon National Park, from the south entrance station, drive north 4 miles to a right turn onto AZ Highway 64. Drive east approximately 8.7 miles where you will see a left turn sign for Grandview Point; continue driving east on AZ 64 for 2 miles where an Arizona Trail sign indicates a right turn onto a gravel road. Drive 1/2 mile on this road to the Grand Canyon National Park - Kaibab Forest boundary. There is an old cabin here. Continue on Forest Road 310 for .8 mile to Grandview Lookout Tower, the trailhead for the Coconino Segment.

From Grandview Lookout to crossing of FR 310 is 9.1 miles.

ARIZONA TRAIL
COCONINO RIM SEGMENT

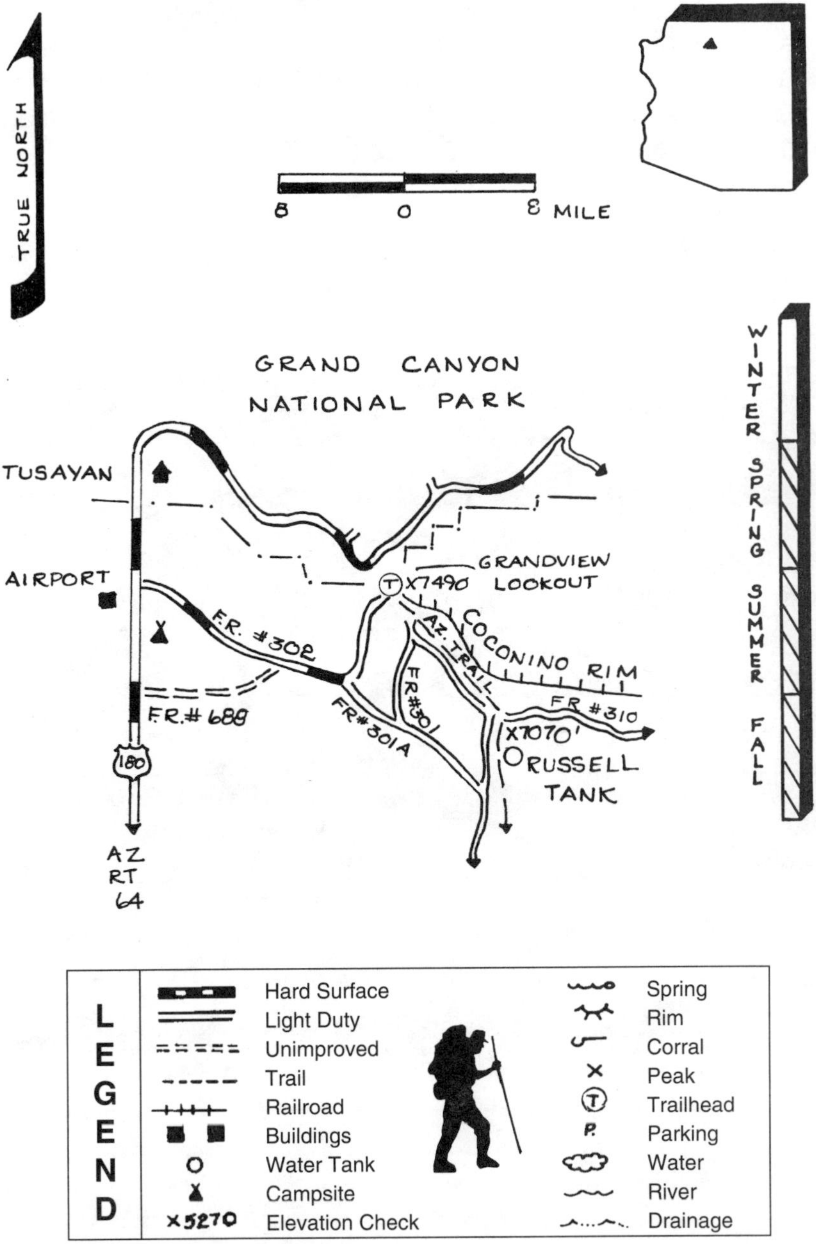

The trail heads east from the tower. The beginning of the trail has an interpretive loop that describes mistletoe and its effects on ponderosa pine forests. It winds through pine-oak woodland with little elevation change. 3.1 miles from the trailhead there is an excellent overlook of the Upper Basin, the Coconino Rim, and the Painted Desert. From here the trail winds closer to the Rim, offering more vistas to the north. A short but steep series of switchbacks begins 7.3 miles from Grandview Lookout, as the trail crosses a steep drainage. At 9.1 miles, the trail meets Forest Road 310. At this point, you are 6.8 miles from Grandview Lookout via Forest Road 310.

Limestone outcrop on the Arizona Trail.
(Photo by John Villinski)

Seeds—waiting for the wind.
(Photos by John Villinski)

Moon over ponderosa pines on the Arizona Trail.
(Photo by John Villinski)

RED BUTTE TRAIL

ATTRACTION: A unique geological formation of the Coconino Plateau, providing an excellent 360-degree view including San Francisco Peaks.

REQUIREMENTS: Water, food, sturdy boots, proper maps; car okay to trailhead; 2.5 hours hiking time round trip.

LOCATION: Tusayan Ranger District, 40 miles north of Williams.

DIFFICULTY: Moderate

ELEVATIONS: 6460' - 7326'

LENGTH: 1.2 miles one way

MAPS REQUIRED: U.S.G.S. topographic 7.5' Quad for Red Butte.

PERMIT: No

BIKES: No - trail is much too steep.

EQUESTRIAN: Yes

WATER: No - bring your own

INFORMATION: Red Butte is sacred to the Havasupai Indians; please treat it with respect. Watch for rattlesnakes in summer.

FIREARMS: Yes

PETS ON LEASH: Yes

TRAIL INFORMATION

Turn off Highway 64/180 onto Forest Road 320. Travel east for 1.5 miles and turn left (north) onto Forest Road 340. After traveling 3/4 mile on this road, turn right (east) onto a spur road; the trailhead is at the end of this 1/4-mile road.

For the first 3/4 mile, the trail climbs moderately and has only a few switchbacks. The last 1/2 mile ascends the steep upper slopes of the butte and has several switchbacks and steep grades. The trail is well marked and easy to follow.

Prepare for a fantastic view of the area.

RED BUTTE TRAIL

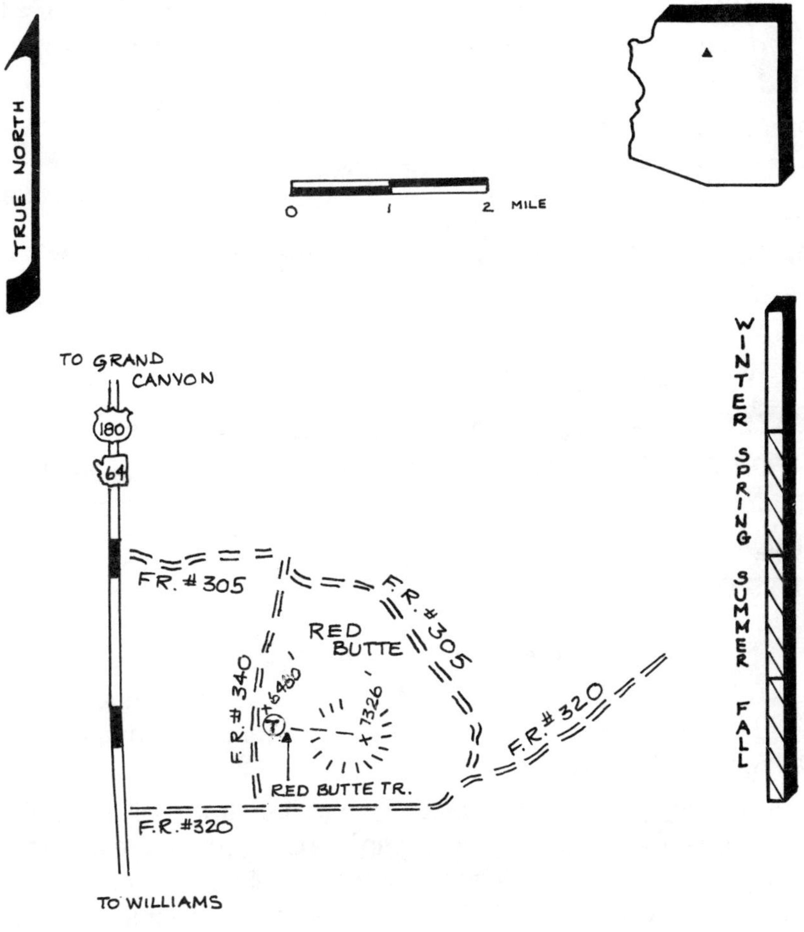

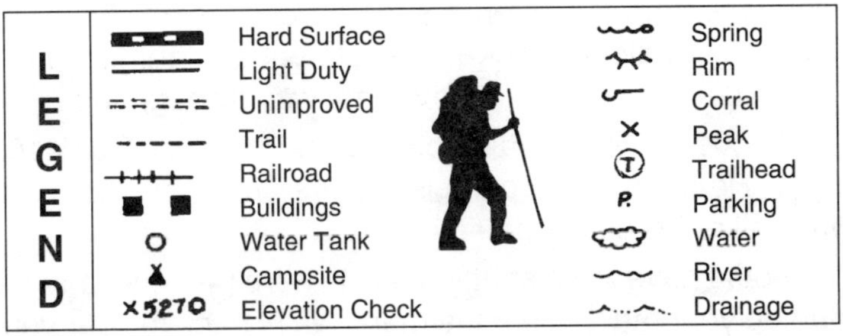

NELSON TRAIL #159

ATTRACTION: Connects with many trails making possible loop hikes, as well as car shuttles.

REQUIREMENTS: Food, water, sturdy boots, proper maps; 4-wheel drive only to trailhead; 4 hours hiking time one way.

LOCATION: Verde Ranger District - Pine Mountain.

DIFFICULTY: Moderate

ELEVATIONS: 5250' - 6100' - 5750'

LENGTH: 8.2 miles one way.

MAPS REQUIRED: U.S.G.S. 7.5 min. topographic for Tule Mesa.

PERMIT: No

BIKES: No

EQUESTRIAN: Yes

WATER: No - bring your own

INFORMATION: Trail access roads are high clearance, 4-wheel drive only.

FIREARMS: Yes

PETS ON LEASH: Yes

TRAIL INFORMATION

Take I-17 north from Phoenix to the Dugas interchange (Forest Road 68), and take Forest Road #68 for 18 miles southeast to the trailhead at Salt Flat.

Just beyond Nelson Place Spring, the trail will enter the wilderness. After following the Sycamore Creek drainage for a little under 2 miles, the trail will head southeast, climbing to its junction with Willow Springs Trail #12. From this point to another junction with Pine Mountain Trail #14, it is short but a bit of a climb. Then you will descend along Bishop Creek to yet another junction with the Verde Rim Trail #161, just over halfway through the hike.

At just over 6 miles is a junction with Pine Flat Trail #165 on your right. Heading west now, it is just under an hour to the end of Nelson Trail at Forest Road #677A.

You could have left a shuttle vehicle here (4-wheel drive) or, if you studied your map, you have many ways back to your vehicle.

NELSON TRAIL #159

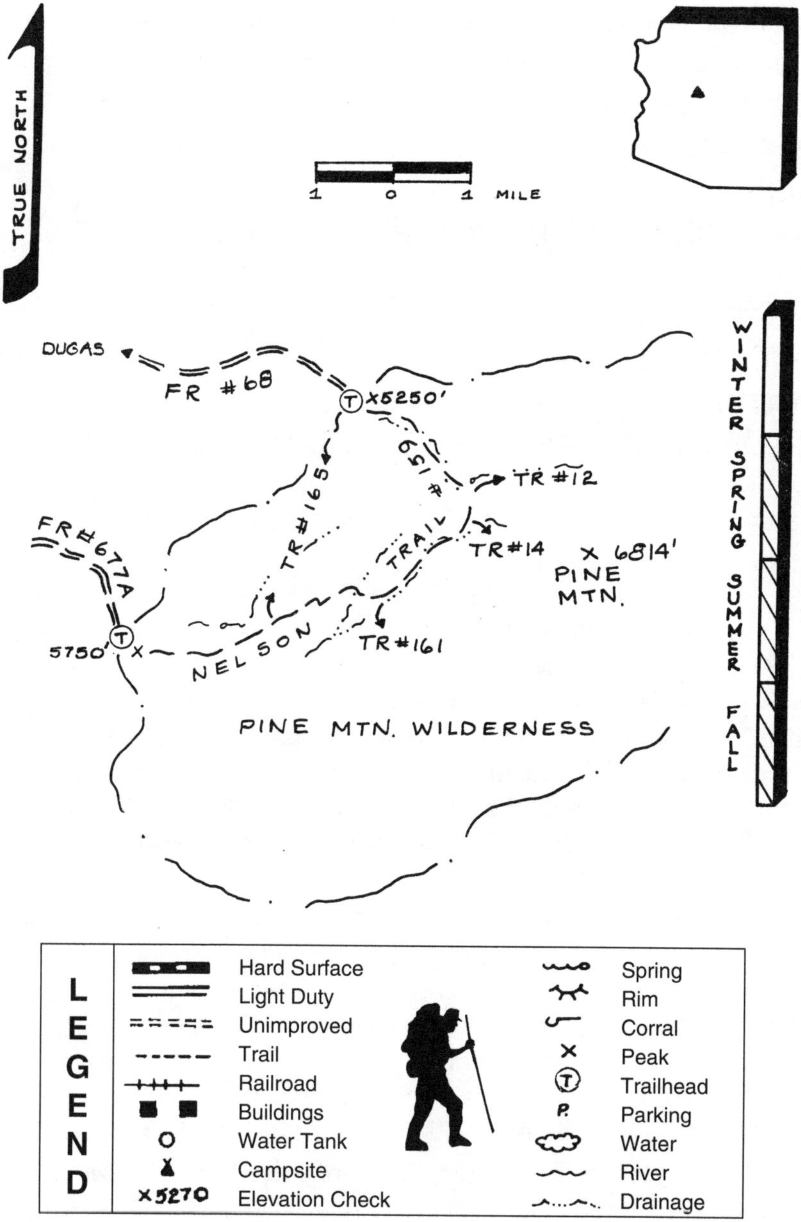

VERDE RIM TRAIL #161

ATTRACTION: Spectacular views of Mazatzal Mountains, Four Peaks and Bradshaw Mountains.

REQUIREMENTS: Food, water, sturdy boots, maps; 4-wheel drive vehicle only to trailhead; 4 hours hiking time one way.

LOCATION: Verde Ranger District - Pine Mountain.

DIFFICULTY: Difficult

ELEVATIONS: 6400' - 6800' - 5700'

LENGTH: 5.3 miles one way.

MAPS REQUIRED: U.S.G.S. 7.5 min. topographic for Tule Mesa.

PERMIT: No

BIKES: No

EQUESTRIAN: Yes

WATER: No - bring your own.

INFORMATION: Steep sections in trail; 2 hours travel time to trailhead.

FIREARMS: Yes **PETS ON LEASH:** Yes

TRAIL INFORMATION

Take I-17 north from Phoenix to the Dugas interchange (Forest Road #68) and follow to Dugas. East of Dugas will be a junction with Forest Road #68G (4-wheel drive), which you will take for 8 miles. On Tule Mesa the road heads southeast; .6 mile past where Forest Road #68G passes under a power line, this road heads, and descends, towards Childs Power Plant. From here Forest Road #9626B (4-wheel drive) heads south for just over 1 mile to the trailhead at wilderness boundary.

You will follow the edge of the Verde Rim for much of the hike. In just over 2 miles, near the junction of Willow Springs Trail #12, you will start a steep climb towards Pine Mountain. In just under 3 miles will be the junction for Pine Mountain Trail #14. Verde Rim Trail only skirts Pine Mountain; if you are up to it, a short steep side trip will take you to the top. The last mile of trail follows Bishop Creek drainage to its end at the junction of Nelson Trail #159.

Check your map for many different ways back to your vehicle or other trailheads where you may have a shuttle.

VERDE RIM TRAIL #161

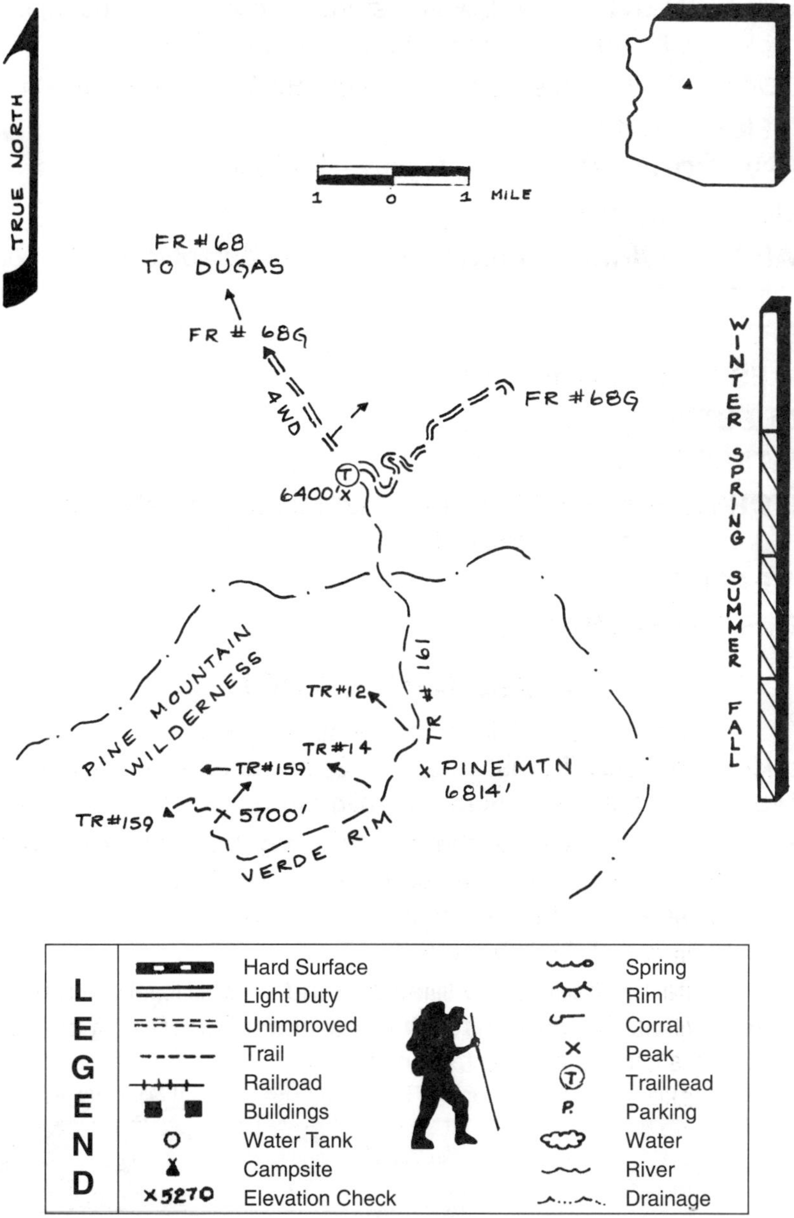

BENHAM TRAIL #38

ATTRACTION: Not a difficult hike with a magnificent view from the top.

REQUIREMENTS: Food, water, sturdy boots, proper maps; car okay to trailhead; 2 hours hiking time one way.

LOCATION: Williams Ranger District - Bill Williams Mountain.

DIFFICULTY: Moderate

ELEVATIONS: 7250' - 9255' to the fire tower.

LENGTH: 4.5 miles one way.

MAPS REQUIRED: U.S.G.S. 7.5 min. topographic for Bill Williams Mountain.

PERMIT: No

BIKES: Not recommended.

EQUESTRIAN: Yes

WATER: No - bring your own.

INFORMATION: Bill Williams Trail #21 makes a fine alternate way down; car shuttle required.

FIREARMS: Yes

PETS ON LEASH: Yes

TRAIL INFORMATION

Take old Route 66 just southwest of Williams. Travel to Perkinsville Road (Forest Road #173) and then to Forest Road #140. Turn right and park at the trailhead.

The trail begins along the north edge of the Benham Ranch property and heads west then south along the lower slopes of Bill Williams Mountain, before some switchbacks that travel up the southwest face of the mountain.

The trail crosses Bill Williams Road in four places before connecting with Bill Williams Trail #21 at about 8800 feet. You may follow Bill Williams Trail to the fire tower.

BENHAM TRAIL #38

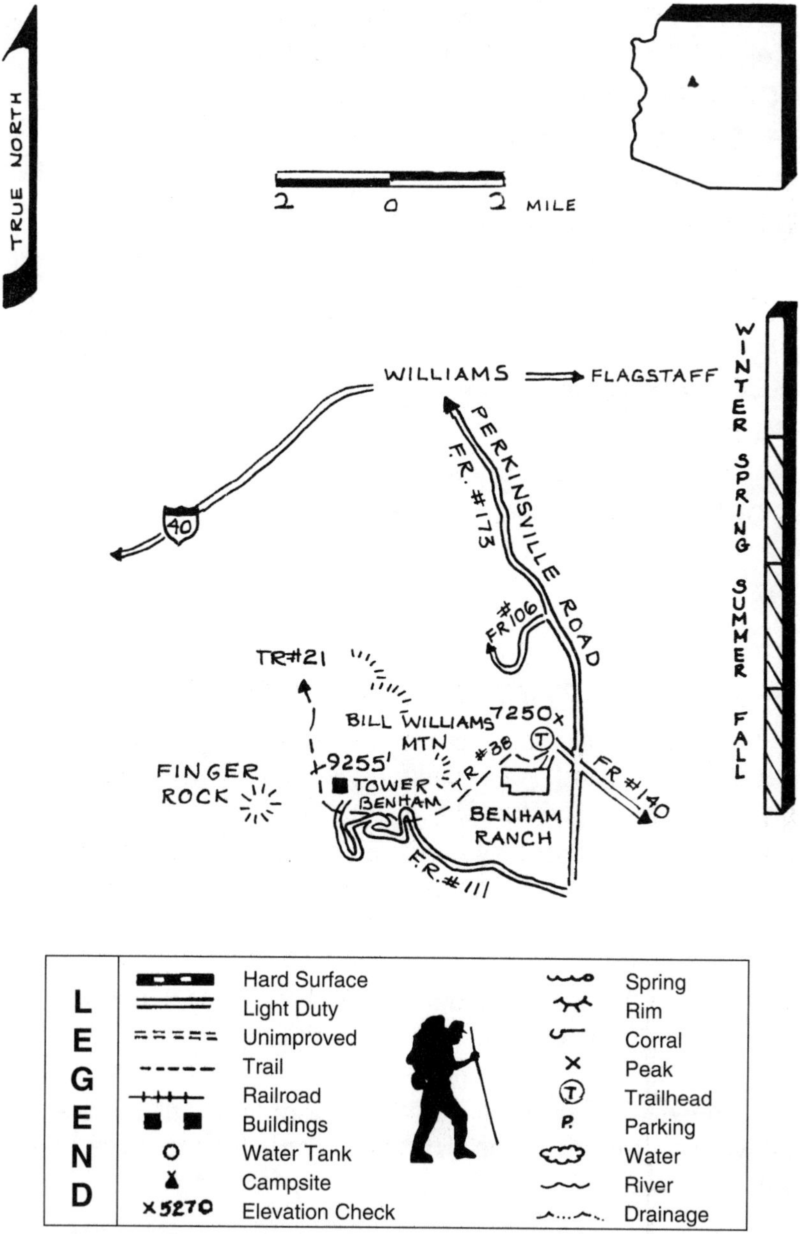

BILL WILLIAMS TRAIL #21

ATTRACTION: A toll was charged from the peak in 1902; now it's free.

REQUIREMENTS: Food, water, sturdy boots, proper maps; car okay to trailhead; 2.5 hours hiking time one way.

LOCATION: Williams Ranger District - Bill Williams Mountain.

DIFFICULTY: Moderate

ELEVATIONS: 7000' - 9256'

LENGTH: 3.5 miles one way.

MAPS REQUIRED: U.S.G.S. 15 min. topographic for Bill Williams Mountain.

PERMIT: No

BIKES: Not recommended.

EQUESTRIAN: Yes

WATER: No - bring your own

INFORMATION: Violent storms and high winds develop quickly on peak.

FIREARMS: Yes

PETS ON LEASH: Yes

TRAIL INFORMATION

In Williams, go west on Bill Williams Avenue about 1 mile, turn left at Clover Hill and proceed along the frontage road to the turnoff to Williams Ranger District Office. Follow the signs to the trailhead.

The trail starts out easy. As you cross West Cataract Creek, it goes through aspens and ferns. Several points along the trail offer good views of the valley below and distant peaks.

Although the trail is well kept, the forest still closes in on you with some of the largest aspen I have ever seen. Up further, the winds begin to increase as the last tenth of the hike gets a little steep.

Three miles from the start, the trail terminates at a gravel road that winds to the top of the mountain. From the top, breathtaking views await you.

BILL WILLIAMS TRAIL #21

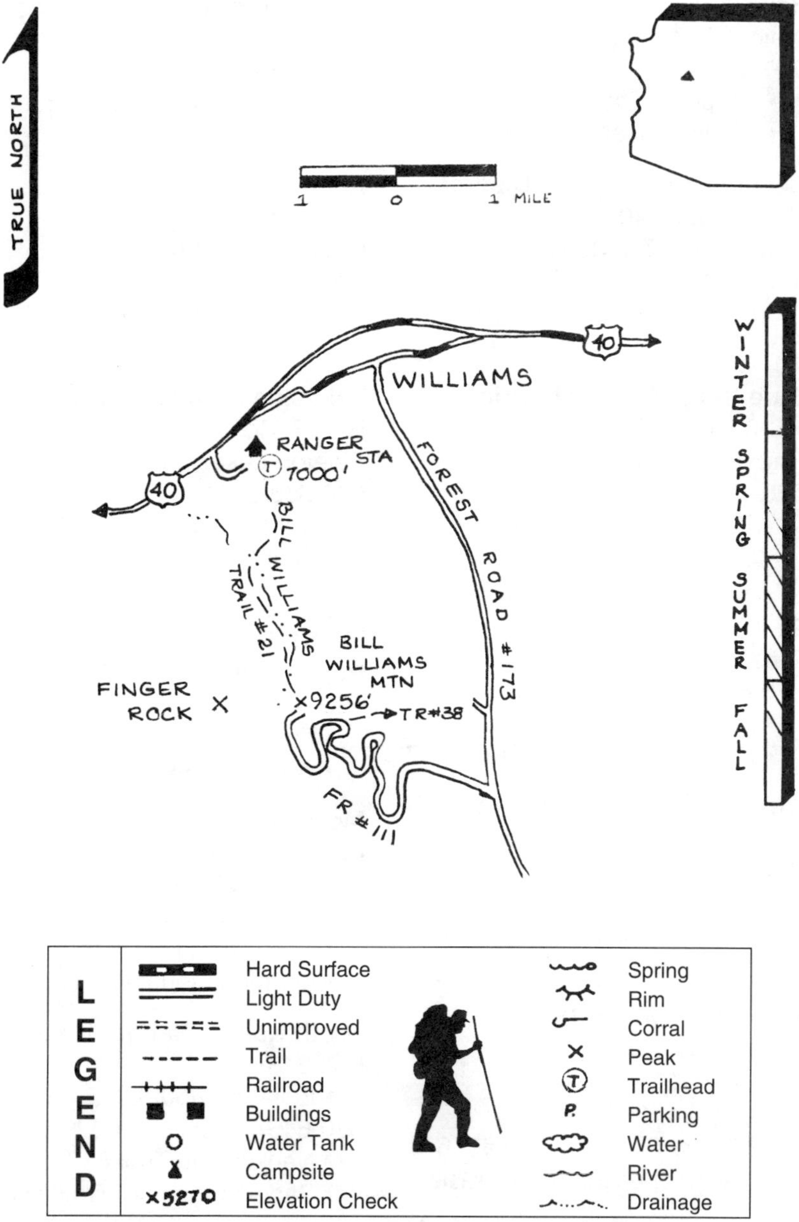

HIKING NORTHERN ARIZONA RANGER DISTRICTS

Contact the following for more information:

Alpine Ranger District
Box 469
Alpine, AZ 85920
520-339-4384
- Escudilla Trail #308
- Steeple Mesa Trail #73

Beaver Creek Ranger District
HC-64, Box 240
Rim Rock, AZ 86335
520-567-4501
- Apache Maid Trail #15
- Flume Road Trail #154

Blue Ridge Ranger District
HC-31, Box 300
Happy Jack, AZ 86024
520-477-2255
- Barbershop Trail #91
- U-Bar Trail #28

Bradshaw Ranger District
2230 E. Highway 69
Prescott, AZ 86301
520-445-7253
- E Cross L Trail #281
- Groom Creek Loop Trail #307

Chalender Ranger District
501 W. Bill Williams Avenue
Williams, AZ 86046
520-635-2676
- Kendrick Mountain Trail #22
- Pumpkin Trail #39

Chevelon Ranger District
HC-62, Box 600
Winslow, AZ 86047
520-289-2471
- Military Sinkhole Trail #966
- Telephone Ridge Trail #103

Chino Valley Ranger District
735 N. Highway 89, Box 485
Chino Valley, AZ 86323
520-636-2302
- Hyde Mountain Trail #6
- Sycamore Trail #63

Heber Ranger District
Box 968
Overgaard, AZ 85933
520-535-4481
- Rim Lakes Vista Trail #622
- Sinkhole Trail

Lakeside Ranger District
R.R. 3, Box B-50
Pinetop-Lakeside, AZ 85929
520-368-5111
- Springs Loop Trail #633
- Timber Mesa Trail #636

Long Valley Ranger District
HC-31, Box 68
Happy Jack, AZ 86024
520-354-2216
- Tramway Trail #32
- Willow Crossing Trail #38

Mormon Lake Ranger District
4825 S. Lake Mary Road
Flagstaff, AZ 86001
520-556-7474
- Lake View Trail #132
- Mormon Mountain Trail #58

North Kaibab Ranger District
Box 248
Fredonia, AZ 86022
520-643-7395
- Nankoweap Trail #57
- Saddle Mountain Trail #31

(Continued next page)

(Ranger Districts Continued)

Peaks Ranger District
5075 N. Highway 89
Flagstaff, AZ 86004
520-526-0866

- Elden Lookout Trail #4
- Heart Trail #103
- Humphreys Peak Trail #104
- Kachina Trail #150
- Little Elden Trail
- Sandy Seep Trail #129

Sedona Ranger District
Box 300
Sedona, AZ 86336-0300
520-282-4119

- Loy Trail #5
- Wilson Mountain Trail #10

Springerville Ranger District
Box 640
Springerville, AZ 85938
520-333-4372

- East Fork Trail #95
- West Fork Trail #94

Tusyan Ranger District
Box 3088
Tusayan, AZ 86023
520-638-2443

- Arizona Trail-Coconino
- Red Butte Trail

VERDE
Box 670
Camp Verde, AZ 86322-0670
520-567-4121

- Nelson Trail #159
- Verde Rim Trail #161

WILLIAMS
R.R. 1, Box 142
Williams, AZ 86046
520-635-2633

- Benham Trail #38
- Bill Williams Mtn. Trail #21

Weather—Great, but Changeable

The saying goes, if you don't like the weather in Arizona, then just wait a few minutes.

This is a fine example of how fast a change can occur and, depending on how far you are out on the trail, and if unprepared, can be the start of your demise.

Arizona's wide array of extremes from the hot arid desert to the cool (if not freezing) lofty peaks carries with it the perfect ingredients for you to be concerned—concerned enough to never travel unprepared!

July and August are the most unpredictable months. Fast growing storms in the mountains and on the desert can cause flash floods and severe drops in temperature.

Always check weather conditions and forecasts before you travel the trails. Again I will stress that you go prepared in every way you can, and be informed!

Trail Etiquette

Let's face it, if you meet someone on the trail, they are there to have a good time and get away from it all, the same as you. If everyone exercises courtesy and cooperation, then everyone has a better time.

Trail etiquette also means having respect for the trail itself. Do not cut switchbacks on a trail. Switchbacks are built to make the trail easier, cutting them only makes your hike harder and causes erosion that damages the trail.

Downhill hikers must always yield to hikers coming uphill, and do it in such a way as to not break their stride or concentration.

If you are hiking faster than the party ahead of you, slow down and wait for them to allow you to pass at an ideal location; thank them.

If you stop for a rest, do so well off the trail, in order to give others a clear path to travel.

Do not hike or ride bikes on wet trails as this activity can cause permanent damage to the trails.

All trail users must yield to all trail stock. These animals can be excitable, and if you are not calm and quiet a rider (or even you) could be badly injured.

If you are allowed a pet on the trail, keep it on a leash. Be careful that you are clear of other hikers so the leash will not trip them.

Loud noises or yelling without reason is distracting to all. Allow others to enjoy the wilderness atmosphere without unnecessary noises.

If we all work together, we can make the great outdoors a pleasant place for everyone, now, as well as in the future.

CONTENTS OF YOUR DAY PACK

Listed below are the items I feel comfortable with. Feel free to add or subtract to suit your needs. Keep in mind that you may be planning a day hike that could turninto an overnite stay for a variety of reasons. Go prepared!

1. Small flashlight, bulbs and batteries
2. Candies that will not melt or spoil
3. Whistle (a police whistle is ideal)
4. Good compass
5. Toilet paper
6. Complete first aid kit
7. Salt tablets
8. Strong sunscreen
9. Any medicines or prescriptions you require
10. Pocket knife
11. Pencil and paper
12. Lighter and waterproof matches
13. Moleskin
14. Lip salve
15. Bug spray for body
16. One day extra food that will not spoil
17. Leakproof canteen and extra water
18. Enough clothing for overnight stay if necessary
19. Plastic bag for litter
20. Raingear
21. Hat
22. Gloves or mittens
23. Sunglasses
24. Maps and Permits
25. Camera and film
26. Identification

I will stress that your maps are valuable only if you study them very carefully before you leave. Be sure you have chosen a hike that is correct for your capabilities.

Let your friends or family know where you are going, when you expect to return and then stick to that plan!

CONTENTS OF YOUR BACKPACK

Backpacks are used primarily for multiple day outings. Be sure your pack is large enough and fits perfectly. Add the following items to your Day Pack List:

1. Sleeping bag and bed roll.
2. Tent
3. Camping stove and extra fuel.

WHAT TO WEAR FOR MOUNTAIN HIKING

In the "Desert Survival" chapter in this book are hints on proper dress for the desert, but mountain dress has a different application. Mountain dress has its variables for lower rolling hills or higher rugged peaks.

LOWER ROLLING HILLS

In these gentle areas, one can use with great comfort the lightweight hiking boots that are popular today. It's not too likely you will need extreme support for lower elevations. Most of these hikes are one-day outings or shorter, so a heavy backpack need not be carried making heavy footgear unnecessary.

Hiking shorts or denim pants work well here, as it is not likely to be cold. I prefer long sleeves and a hat to prevent sunburn. A day pack works well on shorter hikes of this nature. Sweat shirt and raingear are a must.

HIGHER RUGGED PEAKS

In this kind of hiking one must have a very rugged hiking boot, not only for traction, but also for the ever-present need for good support. Some hikers even buy their boots a half size too large, making room for two pair of socks for more comfort. If you do not buy waterproof boots, then at least spray them with one of the products available to help them repel water.

Denim jeans wear well but do not provide much warmth in extreme cold. If you do wear them hiking, then consider carrying a warmer pair of pants and longjohns in case conditions turn colder. T-shirts are most comfortable under your outer shirts. Notice I said "shirts." I find wearing a couple of shirts instead of one heavy one makes it easier to adjust one's temperature by wearing only what is needed instead of too much or too little.

A warm hat, scarf and mittens and heavy jacket should also be carried on these hikes.

WHAT TO DO WHEN YOU ARE LOST OR INJURED

You might think food, water, proper clothing, or even being attacked by wild animals are the most important concerns if you are lost in the wilderness.

However, all of the above are secondary or even immaterial if you do not exercise self-control. If you allow yourself to panic, then indeed you are lost and will probably only be found by accident. Understandably, this situation can instill fear, but do not give in to it!

Don't wander about. Sit down, relax and very carefully try to run through your mind the events that led up to your becoming lost.

If you fail to figure out what went wrong but you still have plenty of daylight left, travel slowly in the direction you feel is correct. Make sure that if you had been climbing that you now travel only downhill.

If you come to a stream, do not leave it unless, of course, you have found your trail. A stream can almost always supply you with water and food and usually leads to civilization as well.

Keep a very close eye on the daylight you have left. If your daylight will soon be gone, you should immediately find a place to camp overnight. Gather whatever rocks or stones are available, place them in a circle to make a place for a safe fire and gather a supply of wood. You should have a fire burning by the time it becomes dark, eaten whatever food you have allowed for your meal and know where everything in your camp is located.

If you cannot build a fire and do not have a blanket or bedroll, then cover yourself with sticks and leaves to escape the cold and wind; it works!

If you are injured and cannot travel, then a signal fire is your best bet. A very smoky fire by day and a bright fire at night has the best chance of bringing results. You can see how important the contents of your backpack or day pack can become.

Again, stay calm! Things can take a brighter outlook in the morning. It has been proven over and over that a clear head can get you out of almost any situation.

Coping with Hypothermia

Hypothermia is a progressive physical and mental collapse that accompanies the cooling of the inner core of the body. It is the primary killer of outdoor recreationists. Symptoms include a feeling of being extremely cold, uncontrollable shivering and incoherent speech.

Getting wet in rain, sleet, snow or heavy fog or even perspiring, along with a moderately cool wind, can start the process at any time or altitude.

More than half your body's heat is lost from your head and neck being exposed. Obviously, then, a good winter hat with ear tabs, along with a scarf, will do a lot to slow down your major heat loss.

Other susceptible areas are your hands and feet. Mittens will keep you hands warmer than gloves, as the air around your hands will act as insulation. Waterproof boots will take care of your feet.

Some rain gear only drapes your upper body and allows your lower pant legs and boots to get soaking wet. A two-piece coat and pants set is better protection.

If you think that you or someone in your party may be suffering from hypothermia, get the person into dry clothes and get a fire started. It is most important to eat. Food will cause your body to develop heat from the digestion process. Administering warm drinks is also extremely beneficial.

If possible, get the person into a prewarmed sleeping bag heated either at your fire or by having someone lie down in it. Build an insulation barrier with leaves, etc., on which to lay the sleeping bag and to keep it out of the wind.

If the patient is going into severe hypothermia, strip him and yourself of clothing and get into the sleeping bag together. There is no faster way to convey body heat.

When planning a hike, think hypothermia. When shopping for hiking gear, when planning your backpack or day pack, think hypothermia!

SAFETY RULES
FOR SURVIVAL IN THE DESERT

(Courtesy Maricopa County Civil Defense and Emergency Services)

1. Never go into the desert without first informing someone as to your destination, your route and when you will return. STICK TO YOUR PLAN.

2. Carry at least one gallon of water per person per day of your trip. Plastic jugs are handy and portable.

3. Be sure your vehicle is in good condition.

4. KEEP AN EYE ON THE SKY. Flash floods may occur any time "thunderheads" are in sight, even though it may not rain where you are.

5. If your vehicle breaks down, stay near it. Your emergency supplies are here. Raise your hood and trunk lid to denote "Help Needed"

6. If you are POSITIVE of the route to help, and must leave your vehicle, leave a note for rescuers as to when you left and the direction you are taking.

7. If you have water — DRINK IT. Do not ration it.

8. If water is limited — KEEP YOUR MOUTH SHUT. Do not talk, do not eat, do not smoke, do not drink alcohol, do not take salt.

9. Do not sit or lie DIRECTLY on the ground. It may be 30 degrees or more hotter than the air.

10. A roadway is a sign of civilization. IF YOU FIND A ROAD, STAY ON IT.

The Desert Southwest is characterized by brilliant sunshine, a wide temperature range, sparse vegetation, a scarcity of water, a high rate of evaporation and low annual rainfall.

Travel in the desert can be an interesting and enjoyable experience or it can be a fatal or near fatal nightmare. The contents of this manual can give only a few of the details necessary for full enjoyment of our desert out-of-doors.

If you think you are lost, do not panic. Sit down for a while, survey the area and take stock of the situation. Try to remember how long it has been since you knew where you were. Decide on a course of action. It may be best to stay right where you are and let your companions or rescuers look for you. This is especially true if there is water and fuel nearby or if there is some means of shelter. Once you decide to remain, make a fire — a smoky one for daytime and a bright one for the night. Other signals may be used, but fire is by far the best.

REMEMBER, MOVE WITH A PURPOSE, NEVER START OUT AND WANDER AIMLESSLY.

Walking: There are special rules and techniques for walking in the desert. By walking slowly and resting about 10 minutes per hour a man in good physical condition can cover about 12-18 miles per day — less after he becomes fatigued or lacks sufficient water or food. On the hot desert it is best to travel early morning or late evening, spending mid-day in whatever shade may be available. In walking, pick the easiest and safest way. Go around obstacles, not over them. Instead of going up or down steep slopes, zigzag to prevent undue exertion. Go around gullies and canyons instead of through them. When walking with companions, adjust the rate to the slowest man. Keep together but allow about 10 feet between members.

At rest stops, if you can sit down in the shade and prop your feet up, remove your shoes and change socks, or straighten out the ones you are wearing. If the ground is too hot to sit on, no shade is available, and you cannot raise your feet, do not remove your shoes as you may not be able to get them back onto swollen feet.

Automobile Driving: Cross country driving or driving on little used roads is hazardous, but can be done successfully if a few simple rules are followed. Move slowly. Do not attempt to negotiate washes without first checking the footing and the clearances. High centers may rupture the oil pan. Overhang may cause the driving wheels to become suspended above the ground. Do not spin wheels in an attempt to gain motion, but apply power very slowly to prevent wheel spin and subsequent digging in. When driving in sand, traction can be increased by partially deflating tires. Start, stop and turn gradually, as sudden motions cause wheels to dig in. There are certain tool and equipment requirements if you intend to drive off the main roads: a shovel, a pick-mattock, a tow chain or cable, at least 50 feet of strong tow rope, tire pump, axe, water cans, gas cans, and of course, your regular spare parts and auto tools.

Clothing: For the desert, light-weight and light colored clothing which covers the whole body is best. Long trousers and long sleeves protect from the sun, help to prevent dehydration and protect against insects, abrasions and lacerations by rocks and brush. Headgear should provide all-around shade as well as eye shade.

Survival Kit: Items that should be carried on the individual are: a sharp knife, a signal mirror, a map of the area, thirty or more feet of nylon string, canteen, matches, a snake bite kit, a firearm and ammunition, and other items that may be useful. Consider carrying your gear in a small rucksack or pack over your shoulders. Weight carried in this manner is less tiring than if carried in pockets or hung on the belt. The pack can be used to sit upon. It also affords a safer method of carrying items, such as the belt knife, hatchet, etc., which may lend to the chances of injury in case of a fall.

Health Hazards: Thought must be given to protecting your health and well-being, and the prevention of fatigue and injury: first, because medical assistance will be some distance away; second, because conditions are usually different and distinct from your everyday living. The desert is a usually healthy environment due to dryness, the lack of human and animal wastes, and the sterilizing effect of the hot sun. Therefore, your immediate bodily needs will be your first consideration.

If you are walking or active, rest 10 minutes each hour. Drink plenty of water, especially early in the morning while the temperature is still low.

While in the desert, wear sun glasses to protect your eyes from glare. Even though the glare does not seem to bother you, it will impair your distant vision and will retard your adaptation to night conditions. If you have no glasses make an eyeshade by slitting a piece of paper, cardboard or cloth. Applying charcoal or soot around the eyes is also beneficial.

In a survival situation everything that you do, each motion that you make, and each step you take must be preceded by the thought: am I safe in doing this?

Keep your clothing on, including shirt and hat. Clothing helps ration your sweat by slowing the evaporation rate and prolonging the cooling effect. It also keeps out the hot desert air and reflects the heat of the sun.

Rationing water at high temperatures is actually inviting disaster because small amounts will not prevent dehydration. Loss of efficiency and collapse always follows dehydration. It is the water in your body that maintains your life, not the water in your canteen.

Keep the mouth shut and breathe through the nose to reduce water loss and drying of mucous membranes. Avoid conversation for the same reason. If possible, cover lips with grease or oil. Alcohol in any form is to be avoided as it will accelerate dehydration. Consider alcohol as food and not as water since additional water is required to assimilate the alcohol. For the same reason, food intake should be kept to a minimum if sufficient water is not available.

Carrying Water: When planning to travel, give your water supply extra thought. Do not carry water in glass containers as these may break. Metal insulated containers are good, but heavy. Carry some water in gallon or half-gallon plastic containers similar to those containing bleach. They are unbreakable, light-weight and carrying several will assure a water supply if one is damaged.

Finding Water in the Desert: If you are near water it is best to remain there and prepare signals for your rescuers. If no water is immediately available look for it, following these leads:

Watch for desert trails — following them may lead to water or civilization, particularly if several such trails join and point toward a specific location.

Flocks of birds will circle over water holes. Listen for their chirping in the morning and evening, and you may be able to locate their watering spot. Quail move toward water in the late afternoon and away in the morning. Doves flock toward watering spots morning and evening. Also look for indications of animals as they tend to feed near water.

Look for plants which grow only where there is water: cottonwoods, sycamores, willows, hackberry, saltcedar, cattails and arrow weed. You may have to dig to find this water. Also keep on the lookout for windmills and water tanks built by ranchers. If cactus fruits are ripe, eat a lot of them to help prevent dehydration.

Methods of Purifying Water: Dirty water should be filtered through several layers of cloth or allowed to settle. This does not purify the water even though it may look clean. Purification to kill germs must be done by one of the following methods:

1. Water purification tablets are the easiest to use. Get them from the drug store and follow the directions on the label. Let stand for thirty minutes.

2. Tincture of Iodine: add three drops per quart of clear water, double for cloudy water. Let stand for thirty minutes.

3. Boiling for 3 to 5 minutes will purify most water.

Food: You must have water to survive, but you can go without food for a few days without harmful effects. In fact, if water is not available, do not eat, as food will only increase your need for water. The important thing about locating food in a survival situation is to know what foods are available in the particular invironment and how to obtain them. Hawks soaring overhead may mean water is nearby. Game will be found around water holes and areas that have heavy brush growth.

Edible Wildlife: Almost every animal, reptile and insect is edible. Learn how to prepare the various things that would be available to you in a survival situation. Avoid any small mammal which appears to be sick. Some animals have scent glands which must be removed before cooking. Do not allow the animal hair to come in contact with the flesh as it will give the meat a disagreeable taste.

1. Jack Rabbit: A hare, with long ears and legs, sandy color. Grubs are often found in the hide or flesh but these do not affect the food value.

2. Cottontail Rabbit: Small, pale gray with white tail. Active in the early morning and late evening.

3. Javelina: Dark gray-black, weighing 30-50 pounds with strong tusks. Has scent glands on the back, over the hind legs. May be dangerous if cornered or wounded.

4. Mourning Dove: Year-round resident, usually found near habitation and water.

5. Gambel's Quail, Scaled Quail, Mearn's Quail: The Gambel's is of primary importance in desert and semi-arid areas.

6. Snakes: Most snakes are edible. Rattlesnake is especially good.

7. Desert Tortoise.

Edible Plants: The main desert edibles are the fruits of the cacti and legumes. All cactus fruits are safe to eat. In the summer the fleshy and thin-walled ripe fruits can be singed over a fire to remove spines. Then they can be peeled and eaten. Old cactus fruits contain seeds which can be pounded between two stones into a powder and eaten, or mixed with water into a gruel. New, young pads of the prickly pear can be singed, peeled and boiled.

The legumes are the bean bearing plants. The main ones are the mesquite, the palo verde, the ironwood and the catclaw. All are small trees with fern-like leaves. All have bean pods which when green and tender can be boiled and eaten. Dry, mature beans, like cactus seeds, are too hard to chew and must be cooked.

In a survival situation, where the use of strange plants for food is indicated, follow these rules: Avoid plants with milky sap. Avoid all red beans. If possible, boil plants which are questionable. Test a cooked plant by holding a small quantity in the mouth for a few moments. If the taste is disagreeable, do not eat it.

Fires and Cooking: Clear an area about 15 feet across, dig a pit or arrange rocks to contain the fire. Make a starting fire of dry grass, small twigs, shavings, under-bark of cottonwoods, etc. Place larger twigs — about pencil size — on top. Have heavier material ready to add, using the small pieces first. Place them on the fire in a "tepee" fashion to prevent smothering your starting fire and aid in the formation of an up-draft. After the fire is burning well, continue to use the tepee method for boiling but criss-cross fuel for forming coals for frying or broiling.

Start your fire with a lighter, matches, or a hand lens. Remember, do not use up your water-proofed matches unless your return from the field is a guaranteed fact. Here are some hints for expeditious fire building.

Drying matches: Damp wooden matches can be dried by stroking 20 to 30 times through the dry hair at the side of the head. Be careful not to knock off the chemical head of very wet matches at the start of the procedure.

Tinder: (All of these must be dry.) Under-bark of the cottonwood, cedar bark, dead goldenrod tops, cattail floss, charred cloth, bird nests, mouse nests, or any readily flammable material shredded into fine fibers.

Fuzz-stick: Cut slivers into soft wood sticks and arrange them tepee fashion with the separated ends downward.

Quick, hot fires: Cottonwood, cactus skeletons, creosote-bush, aspen, tamarisk, cedar, pine, and spruce.

Long-lasting fires: Mesquite, ironwood, black jack, sage, and oak.

REMEMBER, YOU WANT FLAME FOR HEAT, EMBERS FOR COOKING, AND FOR SIGNALS YOU NEED SMOKE IN THE DAYTIME AND BRIGHT FIRES AT NIGHT. BE SURE TO EXTINGUISH YOUR FIRE BEFORE LEAVING IT!

Poisonous Creatures: There is probably more said and less truth about poisonous creatures than any other subject. These animals and insects are for the most part shy, or due to their nature, not often seen. Learn the facts about these creatures and you will see that they are not to be feared but only respected.

Snakes: There are many types of snakes in the southwest but only rattlesnakes and coral snakes are poisonous. Snakes hibernate during the colder months, but will start appearing with the warming trend, sometimes in early February. During the spring and fall months they may be found out in the daytime, but during the summer months they will generally be found out during the night, due to the fact that they cannot stand excessive heat.

Rattlesnakes: These are easily identified by the sandy color, the broad arrow-shaped head, blunt tipped-up nose, and rattles on the tail. Look for them mostly where food, water, and protection is available — around abandoned structures, irrigation ditches, water holes, brush and rock piles. They do not always give warning by rattling, nor do they always strike if one is close. If travelling in areas where rattlers are, wear protective footgear and watch where you put your hands and feet.

Arizona Coral Snake: A small snake, rarely over 20 inches long with small blunt, black head and tapering tail. Wide red and black bands are separated by narrower yellow bands and all completely encircle the body. They are noctunal and live under objects, in burrows, and are shy and timid. Corals bite and chew rather than strike, but due to the very small mouth they are unable to bite any but the smallest extremities.

Treatment of Poisonous Snakebite: If bitten, try to capture the snake as identification will aid in specific medical treatment.

1. KEEP THE VICTIM QUIET AND SEEK MEDICAL HELP.
2. If the "cut and suck" method is deemed necessary, follow the instructions with the snake bite kit. In any event, step 1 above, is very important.

Poisonous Insects and Spiders: The potentially lethal species in this area are the scorpion and the black widow spider.

Prevention and Treatment: In places where venomous species are expected, inspect all clothing and bedding before use, especially items that have been on or near the ground. If bitten (stung), get to a doctor, especially if the victim is a child, is elderly, has a bad heart, or has been bitten several times or on the main part of the body.

Index

A — K

Agassiz Peak 66
Alpine, AZ 12, 14
Apache Maid Mountain 16
Apache Maid Trail #15 16
AZ Trail, Coconino Rim 82
Ash Creek 24
Barbershop Trail #91 20, 22
Battleship Butte 24
Bead Springs Meadow 12
Bell Trail #13 16
Benham Trail #38 92
Bill Williams Mountain 92, 94
Bill Williams Trail #21 92, 94
Black Hills 16
Blue Ridge Campground 20
Blue River 14
Brown Springs Trail #5 36
Calloway Butte 48
Canyon Point Campground 42
Chevelon Canyon 34
Clint's Well 22, 48, 50
Coconino National Forest 20, 22, 38, 48, 50
Coconino Nat'l Forest Tr. #70 38
Coconino Plateau 86
Colorado River 58
Crook's Canyon 24
Dairy Springs Campground 54
Dane Canyon 20, 22
Deadman's Mesa 18
Double Springs Campground 52
Dry Lake Hills trails 70
E Cross L Spring 24
E Cross L Trail #281 24
East Fork Trail #95 78, 80
Elden Lookout Trail #4 60
Elden Mountain 62
Elden Pueblo 62
Encinos picnic area 76
Escudilla Mountain 12
Escudilla Trail #308 12
Fatman's Loop 60
Flagstaff 20, 28, 60, 62, 68, 70, 72
Flume Road Trail #154 18
Fossil Creek 18
Fossil Springs Wilderness. 18
Fred Haught Trail #22 22
General George Crook 32
Goldwater Lake 26
Government Trail 12
Grand Canyon Nat'l Park 56
Grand Canyon Nat'l Park Nankoweap Trail 56
Grandview Lookout Tower 82, 84
Grant Creek 14
Greer, AZ 78, 80
Groom Creek 24
Groom Creek Horse Camp 26
Groom Creek Loop Tr. #307 26
Hancock Ranch 74
Hannagan Meadow 14
Heart Trail #103 62
Highline trailhead 32
House Rock Valley 58
Houston Brothers Trail #18 22
Humphrey's Peak 66, 68
Humphrey's Peak Trail #104 64
Hyde Mountain 36
Hyde Mountain Trail #6 36
Kachina Peaks Wilderness Area 68, 70
Kachina Trail #150 68
Kaibab Forest 56
Kaibab National Forest 82
Kaibab Visitor's Center 56
Kendrick Mountain 30
Kendrick Mountain Trail #22 28
KP Mesa 14
KP Trail #70 14

L — R

Lake View Trail #132 52
Lee Valley Reservoir 78, 80

Little Colorado River 78, 80
Little Elden Trail 62, 70
Loy Butte 74
Loy Trail #5 74
Marble Canyon 56
Midgley Bridge 76
Military Sinkhole Tr. #966 32
Mogollan Campground 40
Mogollon Rim 16, 18, 32, 40
Mormon Lake 52
Mormon Mountain 52, 54
Mormon Mountain Trail #58 54
Mt. Elden 70, 72
Mt. Ord 78, 80
Mt. Union 24
Mud Springs 14
Nankoweap Trail #57 56, 58
Nelson Place Spring 88
Nelson Trail #159 88, 90
North Wilson Trail 76
Oldham Trail 60
Palace Station 24
Payson, AZ 32, 34
Phelps cabin 78
Pine Mountain 88, 90
Pine Mountain Trail #14 88, 90
Pinetop Mountain 36
Pinetop-Lakeside, AZ 44
Prescott, AZ 24, 26
Prescott National Forest 26
Pumpkin Trail #39 30
Quail Spring 24
Red Butte Trail 86
Red Rock Bluffs 38
Rim Lakes Vista Trail #622 40

S — Z

Saddle Mountain Tr. #31 56, 58
Saddle Mtn. Wilderness 56, 58
San Francisco Peaks 16, 64
Sandy Seep Tr. #129 62, 70, 72
Santa Maria Mountains 36
Schultz Tank 70
Secret Mountain 74
Sedona, AZ 76
Senecio franciscanus 66
Sheep Crossing 78, 80
Sheep Crossing Campground 80
Sinkhole Trail 42
Snow Bowl 66, 68
South Spruce Ridge 26
Springs Loop Trail #633 44
Spruce Mountain 26
Steeple Creek 14
Steeple Mesa Trail #73 14
Strawberry, AZ 18
Sunset Trail 62
Sycamore Canyon Wilderness 38
Sycamore Creek 88
Sycamore Trail #63 38
Telephone Ridge Trail #103 34
Terry Flat 12
Thompson Creek 44
Timber Mesa Trail #636 46
Tool Box Draw 12
Trail #165 88
Tramway Trail #32 48
Tule Mesa 88, 90
U-Bar Trail #28 20, 22
Verde Rim 90
Verde Rim Trail #161 88, 90
Verde River Valley 16
West Cataract Creek 94
West Clear Creek 48
West Fork Trail #94 78, 80
Wet Beaver Creek Canyon 16
Wet Beaver Wilderness 16
Williams, AZ 86, 92, 94
Willow Crossing Trail #38 50
Willow Springs Trail #12 88, 90
Willow Valley 50
Wilson Canyon 76
Wilson Mountain 76
Wilson Mountain Trail #10 76
Windsor Tank 52
Winter Cabin 38
Wolf Creek 26
Woods Canyon 32, 34

About the Author

With a degree in Wildlife/Forestry Conservation, it is not surprising that Don Kiefer spends as much time as possible outdoors. Don's books share his experiences and practical knowledge of hiking Arizona.

He has done volunteer work with the National Park Service, recording over 500 hours in the Rincon Wilderness looking for those needing help. The National Forest Service, Pima County Parklands Foundation and Arizona State Parks have also benefitted from Don's services. He has logged over 1,000 hiking miles as a member of the Prevention Walking Society, and an overall total of 4,000 miles of hiking throughout Arizona.

Having learned to fly, Don is especially proud to be an honorary member of the 161st Air Refueling Group at Sky Harbor Airport.

Don began sharing his outdoor world when he started writing for the *Mesa Tribune.* He has now completed five hiking books on Arizona. At the same time, he has been working hard on a hiking library of his own which already consists of 42 volumes, and when complete, will cover every trail in the state.

Don has been cited twice by the National Forest Service and as many times by the National Park Service. He has been honored by B. Dalton Booksellers, as well as Senator John McCain, for his willingness to share his world and his time with everyone. On the wall of Don's office is the Presidential Sports Award received from President George Bush in 1991.

Don is currently working on new hiking books and a book about "haunted" Arizona.

About the Artist

Robyn Wasserman graduated with degrees in Forest Recreation and Natural Resource Management. She has resided in Arizona for 14 years and worked as a park naturalist, hiking guide, fire dispatcher, nursery caretaker and tour guide.

Currently living in Southern Arizona, Robyn is employed as a ranger with Arizona State Parks. When not working, she enjoys hiking, reading, gardening, photography, nature crafts and spending time with her friends.

SNAKES and other REPTILES of the SOUTHWEST

This book is a must for hikers, hunters, campers and all outdoor enthusiasts! More than 80 photographs and illustrations in the text and full color plate insert, this book is the definitive, easy-to-use guide to Southwestern reptiles! By Erik Stoops and Annette Wright.

6 x 9 — 128 Pages . . . $9.95

SCORPIONS and VENOMOUS INSECTS of the SOUTHWEST

A user-friendly guide to the wide variety of scorpions and other venomous creatures of the Southwest. Scorpions, spiders, ticks and mites, centipedes, millipedes, bees and more are shown in detailed illustrations and full color photos. By Erik Stoops and Jeffrey Martin.

5 1/2 x 8 1/2 — 112 Pages . . . $9.95

EXPLORE ARIZONA!

Where to find old coins, bottles, fossil beds, arrowheads, petroglyphs, waterfalls, ice caves, cliff dwellings. Detailed maps to 59 Arizona wonders! By Rick Harris.

5 1/2 x 8 1/2— 128 pages . . . $6.95

DISCOVER ARIZONA!

Enjoy the thrill of discovery! Prehistoric ruins, historic battlegrounds, fossil beds, arrowheads, rock crystals and semi-precious stones! By Rick Harris.

5 1/2 x 8 1/2 — 112 Pages . . . $6.95

HORSE TRAILS IN ARIZONA

Complete guide to over 100 of Arizona's most beautiful equestrian trails, from the desert to the high country. Maps, directions to trailheads, water availability and more to ensure an unmatched experience for all who love hoseback riding. Lodging and "hitchin' post" restaurant information, too! By Jan Hancock.

5 1/2 x 8 1/2 — 160 Pages . . . $9.95